The Land Use Planning System

Evaluating Options for Reform

JOHN CORKINDALE

D1081262

The Institute of Economic Affairs

First published in Great Britain in 2004 by
The Institute of Economic Affairs
2 Lord North Street
Westminster
London sw1p 3lb
in association with Profile Books Ltd

ISBN 0 255 36550 0

Typeset in Stone by MacGuru Ltd
info@macguru.org.uk

Printed and bound in Great Britain by Hobbs the Printers

CONTENTS

THE AUTHOR

Having graduated with degrees in economics and related subjects from Durham and Cambridge Universities, John Corkindale was awarded an overseas fellowship by the Overseas Development Institute and, for two years, managed the development budget for the Ministry of Agriculture, Nairobi, Kenya. On returning to the United Kingdom, he joined the Government Economic Service and worked as economic adviser in various government departments, including the Department of Employment, HM Treasury and the Northern Ireland Department of Finance and Personnel. In June 1988 he joined the Department of the Environment, where he was responsible for economic advice on a range of environmental topics, including sustainable development, agriculture and the environment, and wildlife and biodiversity conservation.

John Corkindale's research on the economics of land use planning dates from April 1995, when he joined the Department of Land Economy, Cambridge, for one year as a visiting government research fellow. On returning to the Department of the Environment, he was appointed economic adviser on land use planning. He has recently been working part-time for the Parliamentary Ombudsman, for whom he has been carrying out a review of policy and practice on redress for maladministration, and for the Open University, for whom he teaches environmental valuation and policy. His green credentials include a long-standing interest in wildlife conservation; for many years he was a volunteer recorder for the Birds of Estuaries Enquiry and for the Wetland Bird Survey. John devotes much of his spare time to furthering his career as an operatic tenor.

FOREWORD

The land use planning system in the UK offends all the principles of liberal economics: decisions about change of use and development are taken by politicians and developers, not by owners; the price system is prevented from playing its proper role in communicating information about the economic desirability of changes to land use; decisions depend not on the balancing of the subjective costs and benefits of a change of use but on who is the victor in a battle between interest groups; and the uses to which land is put are determined by a top-down central planning exercise.

Lest it be thought that this approach is necessary to preserve environmental amenities, it should be remembered that no system of central planning will be able to process the information relating to the costs and benefits of such amenities and therefore there is no reason to believe that environmental amenities will not be under-provided by central planning. Indeed, road congestion is likely to be above optimal levels because road use is not charged; there is reason to believe that development within towns is more dense than is optimal while more rural areas are farmed too intensively and are too sparsely populated; a major developer may well be able to use political influence to undertake development that would not take place if those who, in a free market system, would have property rights in environmental amenities had to be compensated, and so on.

Thus there is every possibility that the current planning system in the UK manages to achieve every adverse result possible, including, *inter alia*, overdevelopment in environmentally sensitive areas; over-optimal road use; underdevelopment; high house prices; over-intensive agricultural use; a lack of environmental amenities (particularly in urban areas); and population distributions that make mass transit expensive.

In Hobart Paper 148 John Corkindale, a former Economic Adviser on Land Use Planning to the Department of the Environment, describes the problems with the system of land use planning in the UK. He then relates those problems to economic theory and shows how economic theory can help develop a better land use planning system.

In fact, argues Corkindale, legislation currently before Parliament can guide us towards a partial solution to the policy problems in this area.

Developers or those wanting to change land use will make economic gains – known as 'planning gain' in the current land use planning system. Others will lose from the development or change of use – and they may have their own fairly, albeit often informally, acquired property rights infringed. The concept of planning gain can be used to ensure that gainers compensate losers.

If this principle is accepted, we can go further. If gainers are to compensate losers, development or change of use will not take place unless it is economically beneficial. Development therefore does not need to be controlled by the local authority. Land use planning and development rights can be 'privatised'. The courts can determine appropriate compensation if there is a dispute.

There is little prospect of legislation currently before Parliament taking us to this destination, even though it does point us in the right direction. Taxation of planning gain will be seen by local authorities as a surrogate betterment tax to be used for their own purposes, not to compensate the losers.

Corkindale accepts that his main proposal will not deal adequately with all situations. In many cases the number of 'losers' may be too big or the amount of necessary compensation too small to allow his proposals to work efficiently. He therefore proposes complementary, market-based measures to sit alongside his main proposal. Nonetheless, the proposals, taken as a package, do have the potential to transform the planning system from a series of battles between interest groups investing economic resources in the political process to a system based on rational agents negotiating mutually beneficial arrangements. As such, *The Land Use Planning System: Evaluating Options for Reform* deserves to be taken seriously by all who have an interest in efficient land use decisions.

As in all IEA publications, the views expressed in Hobart Paper 148 are those of the author and not those of the Institute (which has no corporate view), its managing trustees, Academic Advisory Council members or senior staff.

PHILIP BOOTH

Editorial and Programme Director,
Institute of Economic Affairs
Professor of Insurance and Risk Management,
Sir John Cass Business School, City University
January 2004

ACKNOWLEDGEMENTS

This Hobart Paper develops some ideas set out earlier in Discussion Paper No. 77 published by the Department of Land Economy, Cambridge, in the IEA's Studies on the Environment No. 12, and, in somewhat more mature form, in an article published in the November 1999 edition of the *Journal of Environment and Planning A.* In writing it, I am indebted to anonymous academic referees for helpful comments on earlier drafts.

SUMMARY

- The British planning system is expensive and bureaucratic
  and prevents economically beneficial development – even
  where the gains to developers far outweigh the costs to
  affected parties.
- These problems result from the particular way in which the
  planning system has evolved in the post-war period, but also
  from the flawed principles on which the system is based.
- Under current UK planning law, while the ownership of
  property is generally private, development and change
  of use rights are, in effect, nationalised or municipalised.
  Furthermore, recourse to the courts is not possible unless
  proper procedures have not been followed by the statutory
  authorities.
- A change of land use or development could be regarded
  as a move towards Pareto efficiency if the economic gains
  outweigh the costs to the affected parties and it is possible to
  compensate the affected parties for the impact of the change
  of use or development.
- The concept of 'planning gain' can be used to facilitate
  economically efficient development and change of use by
  ensuring that developers are charged for the costs they
  impose on third parties.
- However, planning gain is frequently used in practice as a

13

surrogate 'betterment tax' – charges to developers can be arbitrary and proceeds are used for general community projects, not to compensate affected parties. Legislation currently before Parliament will not change this – official statements on the matter have frequently been contradictory.

- Developers and those undertaking a change of land use should be required to compensate affected third parties for the costs imposed on them. This would ensure that economically efficient development takes place and would remove the incentive for affected third parties to use the political system to impede beneficial development.

- There would be practical difficulties with this approach. Because all land use decisions would be taken privately, the courts would need to be invoked to resolve disputes about the extent of any compensation. However, this is an important function of courts and they are currently asked to adjudicate on similar matters in related fields.

- A second problem with the proposal is that it does not deal easily with situations where a large number of people are affected by development – for example, the case of large infrastructure projects. In such cases, the transactions costs of compensating third parties could be prohibitive.

- To complement the main proposals, other market-based mechanisms within the planning system would have to be developed. These could include tradable development rights and proposals to tax developers for the externalities caused by their decisions. However, these are second-best solutions and efforts should always be made to compensate losers where possible.

The Land Use Planning System

1 INTRODUCTION

Legislative background

The regulation of land use in the UK has a long history – as early as 1580 a proclamation of Queen Elizabeth I forbade any new building on a site within three miles of the city gates of London (Department of the Environment, 1988a). The system of land use planning in force at the time of writing, however, has its origin in the 1947 Town and Country Planning Acts. There have been many legislative and regulatory changes since the 1947 acts were introduced. In England, the primary legislation governing the planning process is currently contained in three Acts of Parliament: the Town and Country Planning Act 1990; the Planning (Listed Buildings and Conservation Areas) Act 1990; and the Planning (Hazardous Substances) Act 1990. Each of these was amended by the Planning and Compensation Act 1991. Somewhat similar legislation governs the planning process in the other parts of the UK. Nevertheless, despite the legislative changes that have been made since 1947, in essence the system has remained unchanged since that time. The British land use planning system as we know it now is therefore over fifty years old.

There have been some signs recently that a thoroughgoing reform of the planning system is now on the political agenda. Since the election in 1997 of the Labour administration, various different government departments have been responsible for policy on land use planning in England. The first of these was the Department of the Environment, Transport and the Regions (DETR). This was succeeded first by the Department for Transport, Local Government and the Regions (DTLR) and then by the Office of the Deputy Prime Minister (ODPM). Between them these departments have published a series of green consultation papers setting out proposals for the reform of land use planning. The most important of these, referred to hereafter as the planning Green Paper, set out proposals for the planning system generally (DTLR, 2002). A second put forward proposals for the processing of major public infrastructure projects (DETR, 1998). A third, which we refer to below as the planning obligations Green Paper, focused on the particular issue of planning obligations (ODPM, 2002a). Following a period of consultation, on 18 July 2002 the government issued a policy paper setting out its legislative proposals (ODPM, 2002c) and embarked upon legislation in the form of the Planning and Compulsory Purchase Bill during the 2002/03 parliamentary session.

This Hobart Paper comes too late to influence this particular round of legislation. Nevertheless, the publication of the Green Papers and the process of legislation itself have suggested that it would be profitable to revisit the subject of how an economic evaluation of proposals to reform the planning system can usefully be carried out. A number of the proposals floated in the Green Papers were subsequently dropped as a result of the consultation process. Nevertheless, the contents of those Green Papers tells us more about official thinking on land use planning policy than the more matter-of-fact contents of the later policy statement. Our purpose here is to evaluate certain of the proposals set out in these official papers and in the ensuing legislation against the kind of economic criteria developed earlier by the author (Corkindale, 1999). Although no doubt there is much here that, if implemented, might be regarded as progress, the official papers do suffer from certain important drawbacks, as we shall see.

The planning Green Paper identifies various problems with the present system of land use planning. In summary, the planning system is described as 'showing its age'. What was once 'an innovative emphasis on consultation' has now become 'a set of inflexible, legalistic and bureaucratic procedures'. A system that was intended to promote development now blocks it. The slow speed of decision-making undermines productivity and competitiveness in business. People feel they are not sufficiently involved in decisions that affect their lives (DTLR, 2002: 1).

The planning Green Paper identifies two categories of problem: first, the complexity of the planning system and, second, the slow speed and lack of predictability of planning decisions. Examples of particular problems include:

- the multi-layered structure of development plans with up to four tiers of planning;
- national planning guidance that is long and often unfocused;
- rules applying to different types of development that are often unclear;
- a planning appeals procedure with an obscure basis for decision-making;
- decision-making that is both slow and variable between local authorities;
- uncertainty and insufficient clarity about the criteria for judging planning applications;

- drawn-out and expensive processes for updating local authority plans; and
- often slow processes for dealing with appeals against planning decisions and with those planning decisions called in by the central government.

These problems are adjudged by the planning Green Paper to have been depriving the country of the kind of land use planning system needed to plan for a sustainable future. It argues that they have made the planning system the subject of constant attack and its decisions suspect. This in turn has seriously demoralised the planning profession and damaged its ability to recruit new blood. The Green Paper considers that, until there is a clear sense that the system has overcome these problems, it will not attract the degree of public confidence that a good planning system deserves.

The economic evaluation of land use planning

Although the problems identified by the planning Green Paper are no doubt real enough, the paper itself is not underpinned by any serious economic evaluation of the land use planning system. Yet, without it, it is hard to see whether the proposals put forward might represent any improvement on what we have at present. Such economic evaluation is in any case long overdue. The land use planning system is costly in terms of the public expenditure incurred – well over £1 billion per annum – in operating the system, and also in the effect it has on the land and property prices confronting business and private individuals (see, for example, Cheshire and Sheppard, 1989; 1996). Unless there is some evidence that these costs are outweighed by the benefits, it is hard to justify the system. It is also noteworthy that the system of land use planning in the UK, being based on nationalised land development rights, is quite different from that in almost every other country in the world. Yet, despite the length of time the British land use planning system has been in existence, other countries have not seen fit to emulate it. This in itself may not be without significance.

Despite the costs associated with British land use planning, the system itself has not been subject to sustained and systematic evaluation of the kind advocated by economists and other social scientists (B. J. Pearce, 1992). There are at least three reasons for this. The first lies in the very different concepts of evaluation understood by economists and planners (Evans, 1985). Two very different sets of criteria are being applied. The planner's concept of evaluation equates success with the achievement of a planning policy objective regardless of cost. The economist's concept of evaluation, on the other hand, compares the costs and the benefits of a policy in order to judge whether it yields net benefits for society at large. Official guidance on policy evaluation adheres to the latter, economic concept of evaluation (Department of the Environment, 1991; HM Treasury, 2003). The conflict between the two approaches is by no means new. Examples of the kind of problem which can arise are to be found in the reports of the deliberations of official committees, etc., that were created prior to the 1947 Town and Country Planning Acts. These reveal that the members of the committees were much exercised about the problem of urban containment (Royal Commission on the Distribution of the Industrial Population, 1940; Committee on New Towns, 1942; Committee on Land Utilisation in Rural Areas, 1941). For the most part, the authors of these reports elicited a strong preference for urban containment and a rather rigid distinction between the urban and the rural. A criticism of the importance attached to urban containment made at that time was that it was a policy objective that entailed costs and distributional consequences that needed to be made explicit. Questions about how much was to be paid to preserve rural amenities and who was to pay this price were being ignored (Committee on Land Utilisation in Rural Areas – Minority Report, 1941).

A second reason why so little economic evaluation of the planning system has been undertaken lies in the difficulty of measuring the costs and benefits of land use planning, many of which are essentially environmental in character. To date, most progress has been made in the evaluation of individual development proposals using techniques such as community impact evaluation (Lichfield, 1996). Work in this area has been given a stimulus by EC Directive 85/337/EEC on the assessment of the effects of certain public and private projects on the environment. For example, research for the (then) Department of the Environment on how best to implement this directive has, *inter alia*, led to the publication of guidance on the use to be made of environmental (impact) statements in the evaluation of land use development proposals (Land Use Consultants, 1994a, b). Also, there has been some research on the benefits of planning policy, notably on the benefits of green belt policy (Willis et al., 1992; Willis and Whitby, 1985). Nevertheless, despite recent advances in the techniques of environmental valuation, research in this field remains difficult and expensive, and a thoroughgoing evaluation of the costs and benefits of the planning system seems a long way off.

A third obstacle to evaluation of the planning system is to be found in the content of planning policy. Official guidance on economic evaluation generally indicates that the first step in evaluating policy is to define the objectives of policy. Yet it is precisely this first step that the few serious attempts to conduct an economic evaluation of British land use planning have found it difficult to take or to go beyond (Hall et al., 1973; Department of Land Economy, University of Cambridge, 1995). The public policy objectives of land use planning are often not very precisely specified and this tends to make policy evaluation rather difficult. Thus, there has been little explicit attempt to relate the physically defined policy objectives – such as urban containment or the protection of rural land – to fundamental objectives related to the value systems of people (Hall et al., 1973). Equally, although the planning policy guidance notes (PPGs) contain details of a large number of planning policy objectives, these have been criticised for various reasons. For example, they were seen as being of the 'motherhood and apple pie' variety in research carried out by the Department of Land Economy, University of Cambridge (1995). This research concluded that planning objectives were so bland and uncontroversial it was difficult to know why they were included; how it might be possible to gauge whether or not they were being achieved; and what particular role the planning system might have in their achievement.

Against this background, it is not immediately obvious how anyone wishing to carry out an economic evaluation of the planning system should proceed. It has become traditional in the field of economics to distinguish between normative and positive economics (see, for example, Lipsey, 1989). Generally, positive economic analysis takes policy objectives as given and seeks to analyse how they can most cost-effectively be achieved or to quantify the costs and benefits associated with pursuing them. In doing so, positive economic analysis does, on occasion, yield evidence that strongly suggests that changes in policy objectives might be appropriate. Normative economics, on the other hand, goes a step farther; it actually prescribes policy objectives. As such, it might be argued that normative economics takes the economic analyst outside his legitimate sphere and intrudes into the decision-making that is normally regarded as the provenance of politicians. On the other hand, given that positive economic analysis so often yields results that have implications for policy objectives, it is not immediately obvious that what normative economics does is necessarily so outrageous. We would argue that, as the objectives of land use planning policy have been so ill defined, and provided the case is made, it is legitimate for economists to propose changes to them.

In practical terms, there are various options for anyone wishing to carry out an economic evaluation of British land use planning. One possibility is simply to confine oneself to analysing the effects of the planning system on certain variables such as the price of land and houses. A second possibility is to take one of the important and long-standing objectives of land use planning that can be identified and to carry out a partial evaluation of the planning system focusing analysis exclusively upon that objective. One such example might be the long-standing objective of urban containment, a subject we will return to in due course. A third possibility is to adopt a more normative approach and argue for an over-arching policy objective such as 'sustainable development' or 'economic optimisation' for land use planning and to evaluate the land use planning system accordingly. The approach adopted here looks at all three possibilities. First, however, we will describe in more detail precisely what the British land use planning system consists of.

2 THE BRITISH LAND USE PLANNING SYSTEM

The concept of planning permission

The 1947 Town and Country Planning Acts adopted an approach in which decisions on planning applications are made against the policy background of a generalised development plan. The way British land use planning policy operates is through a policy cascade that seeks to convert national aspirations into operational local form through regional planning guidance, strategic plans, area-wide development plans and development control (Grant, 1998). To some extent, perhaps, the lack of clarity in the public policy objectives of British land use planning is a consequence of the way in which a pluralist democratic system seeks to use planning law and to mediate between national and local policy objectives. The system is fundamentally a discretionary one in which development proposals are made 'on their merits' (however defined).

The key to understanding how the 1947 Town and Country Planning Acts work is the concept of planning permission. Generally, under the terms of the acts, anyone wishing to develop land by carrying out a substantial physical operation or by making any significant change to the use of land or buildings must first obtain a licence in the form of planning permission from the local planning authority (LPA). While leaving the ownership of land, in terms of its legal title, unchanged, the 1947 acts profoundly changed the property rights governing land development. In effect, the acts nationalised land development rights and gave the planning authorities the power to reprivatise those rights on a partial and discretionary basis. Compensation for development rights nationalised by the 1947 acts was paid out of a national fund, and developers were, in return, to pay a development charge amounting to 100 per cent of the increase in the value of land resulting from any subsequent development.[1]

1   Development tax has proved to be a political hot potato. The reason is that, as Henry George pointed out in his best-selling book *Progress and Poverty*, published in 1879, the fixed supply of land combined with a rapidly rising demand for it enables landowners to gain from economic progress without necessarily contributing to it. George therefore advocated a land value tax designed to remove the landlords' unearned increment. A further appeal of land value taxes is that, in principle, economic rent can be taxed away without affecting the allocation of resources. There are at least two objections to this line of argument. First, economic rent accrues to other factors of production, notably skilled labour, besides land, and it is not obvious why land should be singled out for special treatment in this respect. Second, there is a practical problem in actually devising a tax system that will tax economic rent rather than the return on capital invested by landowners. When George first put forward his ideas he believed that a land value tax could replace all other taxes and become the sole source of finance for public expenditure. In the twentieth century, this became unrealistic because of the great expansion of public expenditure into areas perhaps not even imagined in the nineteenth century. Today, therefore, a land value tax could only finance a small element of total public expenditure unless public expenditure were reduced; rent from land simply does not account for that much of total factor income. However, what does seem desirable is that, so far as possible, economic rent arising from government land use planning policies that artificially restrict the supply of land should be subject to tax. Arguments of this kind notwithstanding, in 1953 the Conservative administration abolished the development charge, along with the national compensation fund. In 1967, the Labour administration introduced a 40 per cent tax on betterment, but this was again repealed by the incoming Conservative administration in 1971. In 1976, the Labour administration introduced betterment taxation at rates varying from 66.6 per cent to 80 per cent on betterment in excess of £10,000. In 1980, the Conservative administration raised this threshold to £50,000 and introduced a single rate of 60 per cent. In 1985, it abolished the tax altogether, and this remains the position at the time of writing.

Although, under the terms of the acts, the state does not own any physical asset, it does have a right to control development. This right is divested by the grant of planning permission, but this divesting relates only to a specific development proposal, and local planning authorities tend to maintain tight controls over its execution and subsequent use. The local planning authorities and the relevant government minister have a wide measure of discretion as to whether to grant permission and as to the conditions under which that planning permission is granted.

The 1947 acts do, however, place certain limits on the discretionary powers of the planning authorities. They do this in three principal ways by giving landowners certain rights (Grant, 1988). These rights are:

- the right to continued existing use of their land and property, together with any of the (relatively minor) permitted or exempted development rights created by the acts or by the subordinate legislation;
- the right to have any application for planning permission determined by the local planning authority (and, on appeal, by the relevant government minister) in accordance with law, having regard to planning and all other 'material considerations'; and
- the right to make representations in relation to planning applications made by others which may, through externalities, have an adverse impact on one's own property.

It is important to realise, however, that, in exercising these rights, landowners have only limited recourse to the courts. Thus, although landowners have the right to make representations in relation to planning applications made by others that may impact on their own property, there is no right of litigation for this purpose. Also, while it is true that the second right referred to above, namely the right to have planning applications determined by the planning authorities, is enforceable by application to the courts, the role of the courts is, in fact, quite limited. For example, the courts have not seen it as their function to try to establish the proper relationship between the conditions accompanying a grant of planning permission and the projected impact of a proposed development. On the contrary, in the House of Lords judgement on Tesco Stores plc versus the Secretary of State for the Environment (House of Lords, May 1995), responsibility for this task was explicitly abdicated (Grant, 1996).

Under the terms of the Town and Country Planning Acts, the role of the courts is largely limited to that of ensuring that planning authorities have made their decisions about planning applications in accordance with the proper procedures. Considerable importance is attached to consistency in determining the outcome of planning applications. Thus, one important material consideration is whether the local planning authority's development plan policies are up to date and apply in current circumstances, or whether they have been overtaken by events. For example, policies and proposals in the plan may have been superseded by more recent planning guidance. Also, developments since the plan became operative may have rendered certain policies or proposals in the plan incapable of implementation or out of date. The courts may quash a planning decision if there has been a failure to consider a relevant 'material consideration' or if some irrelevant factor has been taken into account. In practice, however, there have been very few occasions on which the courts have said that a particular consideration is not relevant to planning, while many planning decisions have been quashed because of a failure to take account of a material consideration. On the face of it, therefore, what does or does not constitute a material consideration is of some importance for the system of development control, since it is through this concept that limits to public intervention in the land use planning sphere are set (Stephen, 1988). However, it is only a failure to take account of a material consideration, not the precise manner in which account is taken of a material consideration, which will cause the courts to quash a planning decision.

There is rather little statutory guidance on what does, or does not, constitute a material consideration in planning. Guidance on the interpretation of land use planning policy is, for England, set out in a plethora of planning policy guidance notes (PPGs). For England, these are published nowadays by the Office of the Deputy Prime Minister. The general principles governing the operation of the system are set out in Planning Policy Guidance Note 1 (PPG1) (ODPM, 2002b) and its predecessors. This specifies that, in principle, any consideration that relates to the use and development of land is capable of being classed as a planning consideration. Whether a particular consideration falling within this broad class is 'material' will depend on the circumstances. All the fundamental factors involved in land use planning are included, such as the number, size, layout, design and external appearance of buildings, the proposed means of access, together with landscaping, the impact on the neighbourhood and the availability of infrastructure. The guidance on material considerations contained in PPG1 is, in fact, so general in nature that the ability of the courts to limit the discretionary powers of the planning authorities by application of the *ultra vires* doctrine must be seriously diminished (Stephen, 1987).

Furthermore, even when the courts do quash a planning decision because a planning authority has, in the court's view, behaved unreasonably or imposed a condition that fails its tests, the matter is simply returned to the planning authority for further consideration. The courts have seldom severed a condition they have considered unlawful from a grant of planning permission. When a condition of any significance is quashed, it usually means that the whole decision is quashed. The planning authority's right to make a planning decision, therefore, is not abrogated. Where their decision to grant planning permission subject to conditions is quashed, the planning authority might simply decide to refuse planning permission altogether. It is up to the parties – developer and planning authority – to bargain around that entitlement, but the consent of the local planning authority has to be obtained before development takes place (ibid.), and the element of discretion on the part of the local planning authority is retained.

Administrative discretion in land use planning

Recognition that the exercise of administrative discretion can result in inefficiency is implicit in what the planning Green Paper has to say about the lack of predictability in planning. For example, it is stated that the outcome of planning applications is frequently uncertain because there is insufficient clarity about the criteria against which an application will be judged. Moreover, although the current planning system is supposed to be very 'consultative', it too often fails to engage communities. The result is that the community feels disempowered. The reasons given for this apparent contradiction are threefold. First, the procedures that lead to the adoption of a plan can be so protracted that there is a perception that the system favours those with the deepest pockets and the greatest stamina. Second, local planning committees can make decisions on planning applications without the applicants or objectors having an opportunity to present their case. Third, some planning procedures are legalistic, and effective participation tends to demand at least some specialist knowledge and access to professional advice.

It is interesting to speculate on precisely why it is that those who operate the land use planning system seem so wedded to the exercise of administrative discretion. In his comparison of land use planning in the UK with that in the USA, Wakeford (1990) expressed support for the discretionary content of British planning. In his view the British system starts with discretion and introduces some certainty by ensuring that the development plan influences decisions and by providing an appeal process to help achieve consistency in decision-making. This was certainly not the view of Stephen (1987). In his comparison of land use planning in the UK with that in Ontario, he was highly critical of the discretionary content in the British system on the grounds that it is not conducive to clarity in the ultimate objectives of public policy.

The planning Green Paper proposes to address the problems it identified by giving planning 'a new strategic focus'. This is to be achieved by a simplification of the complex hierarchical system of plans and the replacement of local plans with new local development frameworks. These frameworks are to include a clear set of criteria by which local authorities will be able to steer development and to use growth to deliver 'the vision for their areas'. The new system is expected better to engage communities through participation in the preparation of the new local development frameworks and in drawing up action plans that bear on local areas. There is to be clearer information for planning applicants and new requirements for openness and accountability within the planning process.

It is conceivable that these proposals might actually result in a simplification of the land use planning system and in greater openness and accountability in its governance. However, one should not be too optimistic about this. The problem with the proposals is that they do not really address the extent of the administrative discretion within the land use planning system. This deficiency is worrying. As with much else in British land use planning, the extent of administrative discretion within the system has its origin in the nationalisation of land development rights introduced by the 1947 Town and Country Planning Acts. One of the most important arguments against the nationalisation of industry is to do with the inefficiency engendered by arbitrary decision-making. The general arguments against the nationalisation of land development rights are somewhat similar to those against the nationalisation of industry. There are important parallels between the 1947 Town and Country Planning Acts and the nationalisation of industry carried out by the Labour administration of 1945–51. They have to do with the role of the state in the management of economic enterprise. Experience suggests that the state will always be tempted to shield public enterprises from competition and to subsidise their inefficiency for various political reasons (Rowthorn and Chang, 1993). As a result, factor prices become distorted and this leads to inappropriate resource allocation (von Mises, 1949; Steele, 1992). Where land development rights are nationalised, the arbitrariness and lack of transparency inherent in the exercise of administrative discretion over the granting of planning permission are likely to result in a pattern of land development that is economically inefficient. Despite the system of development plans, it will not always be clear precisely what governs decisions on whether planning applications are granted or rejected, or what governs the terms under which planning permission is granted. Where the policy objectives of land use planning are so ill defined, as in Britain they are, the desirability of using land in an economically efficient manner is always in danger of being lost sight of completely.

Just as the privatisation of industry during the Conservative administration of 1979–97 has, with the possible exception of the railways, yielded substantial efficiency gains, so we would argue that privatisation of land development rights has the potential to yield efficiency gains too. Under private ownership of industry, enterprises are exposed to competition and resources are allocated more efficiently. Private owners of industry and land development rights also respond to the information contained in price signals so that resources will be allocated to their most valued use. At the same time, the ends of public policy can be served in a transparent manner through regulation and public subsidy. Thus the programme of privatisation embarked upon by the Conservative administration of 1979–97 was accompanied by the introduction of a series of public regulatory agencies. It also provided for public subsidy to be paid out in pursuit of non-commercial, public policy objectives. Similarly, if land development rights were privatised, the regulatory aspects of privatisation would be an important focus of reform.

The comparison between the privatisation of nationalised industries and of nationalised land development rights should not, of course, be pushed too far. The privatisation of land development rights would not, for example, entail the transfer of physical assets. The principal effect of privatisation of land development rights would be to make the criteria for acceptance or rejection of planning applications, and the terms under which planning permission was granted, explicit and subject to judicial review. In the design of such a regulatory framework, the key question for British land use planning policy would be to determine how best to combine the efficient internalisation of externalities generated by land development with public policy objectives such as betterment taxation. More prosaically, the problem would be how best to maintain a sensible balance between the interests of private landowners and the wider concerns of public policy. These questions will be addressed further below. First, however, we examine the implications of recent attempts by government to make sustainable development central to land use planning.

3 SUSTAINABLE DEVELOPMENT AND ECONOMIC OPTIMISATION

Sustainable development and sustainability

According to the planning Green Paper, 'we need good planning to deliver sustainable development, to harness growth to build a better future' and 'we need a better, faster, more accessible system that serves both business and the community' (DTLR, 2002: 1). No one could seriously object to the second of these two aspirations; it falls into the category of 'motherhood and apple pie'. It is also concerned about means rather than ends. On the other hand, the first sentence is of interest in that it purports to make sustainable development *a*, if not *the*, central objective of land use planning. This is also true of the latest version of Planning Policy Guidance Note 1, which sets out the general policy and principles of planning (ODPM, 2002b).

Sustainable development is a public policy objective of a strategic kind. The concept has generally been considered to imply a degree of redistribution of wealth between the present generation and future generations. Planning policy guidance in the UK has been revised in recent years 'in the light of sustainable development'. For example, guidance on how 'to preserve natural capital for the benefit of future generations' is increasingly finding its way into planning guidance. However, it is by no means clear that the concept of sustainable development can bear the weight of policy development that is currently being placed upon it.

Ever since the publication of the report by the World Commission on Environment and Development in 1987 there has been a good deal of political steam behind the concept of sustainable development. At the Toronto summit in June 1988 the then Prime Minister, Mrs Thatcher, joined with her fellow heads of government in endorsing the concept. The following month saw the publication of a report by the then Department of the Environment (1988b) that expressed uneasiness about the policy implications of sustainable development. The second chapter of this publication opened with the following statement:

> The Report [of the World Commission on Environment and
> Development] defines sustainable development as meeting
> the needs of the present without compromising the ability
> of future generations to meet their own needs. There can
> be no quarrel with this as a general definition. The key
> point is how to translate it into practice, how to measure it,
> and to assess progress towards its achievement. This is an
> area which needs to be tackled and on which international
> consensus is desirable in order to develop a consistent
> approach and agreement on what is being achieved.

Since that time, a good deal of effort has gone into the problem of refining the concept and giving it operational significance. This effort has not been very successful, at least in the field of land use planning. Although the PPGs, including PPG1, have been revised 'in the light of sustainable development', it often appears as if these revisions take the form of little more than a liberal scattering of the words 'sustainable development' through documents that, in other respects, remain largely unchanged from earlier versions.

One important and influential attempt to put flesh on the bones of sustainable development is contained in the well-known publication *Blueprint for a Green Economy* (Pearce et al., 1989). 'Blueprint', as it has become known, is in fact an abridged version of a research report commissioned by the Department of the Environment precisely in order to try to address the problems identified in its own report of the previous year. 'Blueprint' popularised the distinction between what it described as 'strong sustainability' and 'weak sustainability'. Both concepts embody the idea of sustainable development as providing a constant capital wealth bequest to future generations and are rooted in notions of intergenerational equity. Under strong sustainability, this wealth bequest is defined as being purely in terms of natural capital, whereas, under weak sustainability, the wealth bequest is defined as comprising a mix of natural capital and man-made capital.

The whistle was blown, so to speak, on these sustainability concepts by a later, almost equally well-known, publication entitled *Small Is Stupid: Blowing the Whistle on the Greens* (Beckerman, 1995: 128). This had no difficulty in drawing attention to the impossibility of pursuing policies based on strong sustainability. Using the beetle as an example of what would have to be conserved under strong sustainability, Professor Beckerman rejects the objective of strong sustainability as morally repugnant: 'Given the acute poverty and environmental degradation in which many of the world's population live, we could not justify using vast resources in an attempt to preserve from extinction, say, every single one of the millions of species of beetle that exist.'

Perhaps more importantly, Beckerman also draws attention to the fact that, once natural and man-made capital are accepted as being to some extent interchangeable, there is essentially no difference between weak sustainability and what he describes as 'the old fashioned economist's concept of economic optimisation'. Weak sustainability allows for the possibility of some natural resources being run down so long as there is an adequate increase in other resources, including those in the form of man-made capital. In other words, weak sustainability allows for substitutability between different forms of natural capital and man-made capital, provided there is no overall decline in human welfare. However, on this view, if the choice between preserving natural capital and adding to man-made capital depends on which makes the greater contribution to human welfare, the concept of sustainability, and with it the concept of sustainable development, becomes redundant.

The distinction between weak sustainability and strong sustainability was taken a stage farther by Gibbs et al. (1998), who identify a spectrum of perspectives from technocentric 'very weak sustainability' to ecocentric 'very strong sustainability'. This further refinement makes no difference to the veracity of Beckerman's argument. However, it has helped contribute to the view that, since the concept of sustainable development is so much open to interpretation, it can easily degenerate into a bargaining device to be used by sectional interests in pursuit of their own goals (Tate, 1994). This has not deterred Adams and Watkins (2002) from reviewing whether sustainable development does or does not support the case for the compact city. They draw attention, on the one hand, to arguments that sustainable development demands a reversal of the processes of urban dispersal and a replacement of the policy of mere urban containment by one of urban compaction. On the other hand, they point to arguments suggesting it is doubtful that compact urban forms are achievable in the modern age and that, in any case, urban compaction is not necessarily sustainable or desirable. We do not find this to be an especially helpful debate because, with Beckerman, we do not believe the concept of sustainable development is a sufficiently robust one to bear the weight of such arguments.

Renewable and exhaustible resources

As it happens, in one area the concept of sustainability does have a precise meaning. This is in relation to the exploitation of renewable resources. If renewable resources are harvested at a rate in excess of their maximum sustainable yield, in due course they will become extinct. The economically optimal rate of harvesting of a renewable resource may be higher or lower than the maximum sustainable yield. However, for exhaustible (or non-renewable) resources, the concept of maximum sustainable yield has no meaning (although exhaustible resources can, in a sense, be enhanced through the discovery of new deposits or through technological advances that make it easier to recover a resource from low-grade materials). Thus it makes sense to talk about the economically optimal exploitation of exhaustible resources but not about their sustainable exploitation. The conclusion is that sustainability should be interpreted purely as a technical characteristic associated with the exploitation of renewable resources and not as implying any moral injunction or overriding criterion of choice.

For most of the purposes generally understood as being covered by land use planning, it is more appropriate to think of land as an exhaustible rather than as a renewable resource. For example, much of the debate about urban containment and the desirability of using brown field rather than green field sites for new land development tends to be predicated on the assumption that land, once developed, will always remain developed. In fact this is something of an exaggeration; in principle, there is no reason why urban land should not be returned to something approaching its former pristine rural state. Unfortunately, however, such changes do tend to take a long time and to be rather expensive to achieve. This is not to say that derelict urban land cannot, or on occasion should not, be recycled for essentially rural purposes like recreation, nature conservation or even agriculture. However, it seems unlikely that this will ever be the rule.

Economic optimality as a land use planning objective

If sustainable development is to be the central strategic objective of land use planning, what are the implications? If, with Beckerman, one rejects the pursuit of strong sustainability as unrealistic and considers that the pursuit of weak sustainability is in essence no different from the pursuit of economic optimisation, what does this imply for land use planning? One possible answer is that sustainable development should not be defined in terms of sustainability at all. The difficulty with this argument is that nobody has yet proposed a more convincing way of defining sustainable development. There is really no escaping from the unsatisfactory nature of the concept. If a strategic objective for land use planning is required, the inescapable implication of Beckerman's analysis is that sustainable development is conceptually redundant and that economic optimisation should be substituted for sustainable development as the strategic objective of land use planning. Is this the way British land use planning should go? This is a normative question and, as such, one to be decided upon ultimately by politicians and other decision-makers rather than by mere economic analysts. It is always open to decision-makers to pursue strategic objectives other than economic optimisation; equity in the distribution of income and wealth is one obvious possibility. However, it is not obvious from the planning Green Papers, or indeed from other official sources on land use planning, that this is what their authors have in mind.

In retrospect, it can be seen that there was a large element of 'reinventing the wheel' about the Brundtland Commission's deliberations. Given the concept's lack of conceptual precision, one might well question whether the political steam behind sustainable development is altogether desirable. On the other hand, this political steam has been partly responsible for promoting the recent revival of interest, first, in environmental valuation research and, second, in the use of market-based instruments for environmental policy purposes. In a recent address, Professor Pearce himself was of the view that, since the publication of *Blueprint for a Green Economy* and of the 1990 environment White Paper, it had become commonplace to speak of market-based instruments, environmental valuation and the like (D. Pearce, 2002). There seems little doubt that the publication of *Blueprint for a Green Economy*, in trying to address the problem of what sustainable development was all about, almost inadvertently triggered off these developments. Yet these developments sit far more comfortably with a strategic objective of economic optimisation than they do with one of sustainable development. Moreover, debates about the desirability or otherwise of the compact city, mixed use development, etc., cannot be conducted in a sensible manner without some criterion against which 'desirability' can be assessed. We would argue that the criterion of economic optimality is, in principle, able to provide this, whereas sustainable development cannot.

Decision rules for optimal resource allocation

The concept of economic optimality was not actually invented by Adam Smith, but his notion of the 'invisible hand' described in *The Wealth of Nations* carries with it the idea of the operation of the market as the way to higher living standards (Smith, 1776). Discussion of how the operation of the market would need to be modified, for example to take account of environmental externalities so as to achieve economically optimal outcomes, came later. The construction of the theoretical framework describing the decision rules for optimal resource allocation need not detain us. The interested reader can refer to standard texts on general equilibrium and welfare economics (see, for example, Baumol, 1965). However, before moving on, it is worth drawing attention to two major difficulties in applying these decision rules. First, there are problems of obtaining the right kind of data. For example, economic optimality is not only concerned to take account of market transactions. On the contrary, if land development, for example, results in environmental externalities such as pollution of water or other forms of environmental degradation, these are matters that have to be taken account of, and, ideally, quantified. Such data requirements imply the need for environmental impact assessment to measure physical impacts on the environment. They also imply the need for environmental valuation in order to enable decision-makers to compare such environmental impacts with the other costs and benefits associated with land development.

Second, the decision rules for optimal resource allocation carry with them some important assumptions about the distribution of income and wealth. For example, the rules tend to imply that the existing distribution of income and wealth is as it should be. One consequence is that the wealthy will always have more command over resources than the poor. A variety of possible approaches to this subject have emerged in the literature. For example, there are those authors who virtually ignore the matter. There are those who accept, implicitly or explicitly, that the distribution of income and wealth is as it should be. There are those who argue in favour of a social welfare function based on the assumption that the less inequality there is in society the better. Another approach is to argue that policies should only be adopted provided that they adversely affect nobody at all. In other words, however much some may gain, say, from the implementation of a particular land development proposal, such a proposal should be rejected if there are others who are going to lose by it. This is the approach embodied in the Pareto criterion (Pareto, 1927). It is our belief that adherence to this criterion would potentially be of great help in overcoming disputes about land development.

In exploring the implications of adopting economic optimality as the strategic objective of land use planning, it is these two problems above all others which have to be addressed. The environmental externalities associated with land development are, arguably, the main reason why land use planning policy is needed at all. Without them, there would be no real objection to allowing the market to determine how, where and when land is developed. That this is clearly not the case means that it is incumbent on those advocating market solutions to find ways in which the problem of externalities may be satisfactorily resolved. We will return to this subject in the next section. First, however, we will examine some problems associated with the Pareto criterion.

The Pareto criterion and Pareto improvements

The literature on economic optimisation has gradually developed to embrace the idea of Pareto optimality. Pareto optimality requires that, in order to achieve economic efficiency in the allocation of resources, it must not be possible to change the existing resource allocation in such a way that someone is made better off while leaving no one worse off. The Pareto criterion, on the other hand, specifies that only when at least one person has been made better off and no one worse off can a Pareto improvement in allocative efficiency be said to have occurred. It could be argued that, if one person is made worse off as a result of externalities from a development, their legitimate property rights have been undermined, and the Pareto criterion protects those rights by preventing such development or requiring compensation.

The Pareto criterion is perhaps most widely associated with cost–benefit analysis. Unfortunately, since about the time of the Second World War, it has tended to be rejected by cost–benefit analysts in favour of the so-called Hicks–Kaldor criterion (Hicks, 1939; Kaldor, 1939). Cost–benefit analysts tend to prefer Hicks–Kaldor on the grounds that the Pareto criterion is too restrictive to have much practical application. The Hicks–Kaldor criterion requires that, for a project to receive a green light in cost–benefit analysis, it must be possible to show that the potential gainers are able to compensate the potential losers in full and still be left with some gain. It does not require that compensation actually be paid. The principal criticism of Hicks–Kaldor is that, unless this compensation is actually paid, it will offend against the requirements of Pareto (Baumol, 1965). Unfortunately, this has not, for example, deterred HM Treasury from incorporating the Hicks–Kaldor criterion in its 'Green Book' on appraisal and evaluation (HM Treasury, 2003).

It is this requirement of the Pareto criterion for economic optimality that gainers actually compensate losers that has important implications for land use planning policy. The concept of planning gain – to be discussed further below – might, in principle, be regarded as a means by which third parties can be compensated for the damage associated with the externalities generated by land development. Perceived in this way, it is a rather blunt instrument, the main deficiency of which is that there is no guarantee that individual losers from land development will receive any meaningful compensation at all. The problem of compensating losers from land development is perhaps most obvious in the case of major infrastructure projects. Very often such projects are so large that their economic and environmental impacts are regional or even national in scope. The various proposals for airport expansion in south-east England are a case in point.

The need to find a solution to the problem of the perceived need for airport expansion in the south-east is of course by no means new. As long ago as July 1953 the government of the day published a White Paper setting out the airport situation in the London area as it was at the time (HM Government, 1953). Perhaps the most serious study of the problem came with the publication of the Roskill report (Commission on the Third London Airport, 1971). It became fashionable among some who should have known better to deride the Roskill report for some of the crude environmental valuation contained in it, not least that relating to Norman churches (see, for example, Grove-White, 1997). However, a far more serious criticism of Roskill is that it did not adhere to the requirements of the Pareto criterion. In consequence, there was an immense amount of political opposition, not only to airport expansion at Stansted but also to the development of Cublington, the preferred option of the commission. It is of course quite possible that, had Roskill addressed the practical problems of how to compensate the losers from a development at either site, they would have been found to be insuperable. In the event this was not even attempted, and one might well argue that it was this deficiency which was ultimately responsible for undermining the Roskill Commission's recommendations, including the rejection of its preferred site, namely Cublington, for a third London airport. The Conservative administration of the day instead opted for Foulness Island, as recommended 'on planning grounds' in the minority report to Roskill. This decision was then overturned by the incoming Labour administration in 1974 on grounds of cost. The main consequence has been further expansion at Heathrow and at Stansted. The expansion at Stansted can be seen as ironic in view of the fact that it was political opposition to expansion at Stansted that caused the Roskill Commission to be set up in the first place.

Recognition in the USA of the compensation problem has been one of the factors giving rise to the growth of environmental dispute resolution (Susskind and Cruikshank, 1987). To this extent, proposals for mediation in planning disputes that are contained in the planning Green Paper are welcome. However, neither these proposals nor those for the reform of planning inquiries in our view go far enough in the direction of giving explicit recognition to the need to address the problem of compensating losers from land development. Yet without this the conditions for Pareto efficiency cannot even begin to be achieved. Perhaps more to the point, we would argue that it is only by ensuring that the beneficiaries from land development adequately compensate the losers that the political steam can be taken out of the planning of large-scale infrastructure projects.

One possible way to address the need to find ways for gainers from public infrastructure projects to compensate losers might be to change the terms of reference of planning inquiries. The planning inquiry would then become a forum where potential developers might negotiate with third parties specifically about the form and extent of compensation for environmental externalities. However, changing the role of the planning inquiry in this way is only one of a number of means by which the kind of trade and negotiation necessary to achieve adherence to the Pareto criterion might be achieved. It is time therefore to turn to the more general question of the ways in which this kind of trade and negotiation might be conducted. The starting place for this is the relationship between the economics of environmental externalities and the law of private property rights.

4 THE NORMATIVE THEORY OF PROPERTY

Externalities and property rights

Economic optimality is primarily concerned with questions of economic efficiency. As we have seen, one of the conditions for economic optimality is that there should not be divergence between private and social costs and benefits. In other words, environmental and other externalities[1] have to be internalised if the conditions for economic optimality are to be met. Thus, where a development in land use imposes costs on third parties, steps should ideally be taken to ensure that such third parties are compensated. As we have seen, the discretionary powers of the planning authorities under the 1947 Town and Country Planning Acts are limited

---

1 The terms 'externality', 'external cost' and 'spillover' are used interchangeably in the literature. It is usual to distinguish between pecuniary and technological externalities (Viner, 1931), especially in the context of land use. Pecuniary externalities entail a re-evaluation of assets and a redistribution of economic rents resulting from competitive pressures as old enterprises are replaced by new ones: there is little economic case for addressing these in the planning system, although business may well, in practice, try to prevent competitors setting up, using the planning process. Technological externalities, on the other hand, entail real resource losses, for example through physical damage caused to neighbouring buildings during the construction process. Technological externalities, unlike pecuniary externalities, are directly relevant to the economic efficiency with which productive resources, including land, are used. Land use policy should therefore favour the cost-effective internalisation of technological externalities (Stephen, 1987).

in various ways. In relation to externalities a landowner has the right to make representations in relation to planning applications made by others that may have an adverse effect on his property. By comparison with the position elsewhere in the world, this right is a limited one. In particular, there is only a limited recourse to the courts. This omission is serious. To understand why, it is necessary to examine the important function of the law in establishing a proper relationship between externalities and property rights.

The law has a key role to play in the delineation of property rights and in securing allocative efficiency in the use of scarce resources. Differing conditions can give rise to different property rights regimes, even at the same time and within the same country. For example, in the USA, there are two distinct legal doctrines that govern the use of water. In the eastern states, the prevailing system, which derives from English law, is riparian, permitting landowners reasonable use of the water from rivers that run by their properties. In the western states, which are more arid and where water has a correspondingly higher value, water rights are more thoroughly delineated and the prevailing system is appropriative, granting individuals rights to water (Barzel, 1989). In general, the greater the scarcity of water, the greater its value. Also, the more it will be worth spending money on monitoring and enforcement, the closer it will come to several property.

In countries such as England that operate under the common law, court rulings serve as precedents for similar cases and litigants are, therefore, in effect, helping to resolve others' disputes. While precedent allows the law to achieve some measure of uniformity and provides a degree of certainty over the likely outcome of a case, the common law nevertheless remains flexible in the face of changing economic, social and technological conditions. Precedents are often set by the courts as a result of litigation between parties all of whom may be genuinely uncertain of the legal considerations governing the dispute between them. Where such uncertainty does not exist, it will often be possible to settle a dispute before it reaches court, thus saving substantial legal costs.

Against this background, the question arises as to how the system of development control can be evaluated. As the Green Paper observes, the planning rules applying to different types of development and the basis for decision-making about planning appeals are obscure and unclear (DTLR, 2002). For policy evaluation purposes, what is needed is a set of decision rules against which government policy on the delineation and enforcement of property rights can be assessed. The starting point for this is the normative economic theory of property. Two fundamental normative principles of property law have been identified (Cooter and Ulen, 1988):

- structuring the law to minimise the harm caused by failures in private agreements – the normative Hobbes theory; and
- structuring the law so as to minimise the impediments to private agreements – the normative Coase theory.

The normative Hobbes theory derives from the fact that voluntary exchange and trade are beneficial, but that, as Hobbes argued in his seventeenth-century work *Leviathan*, if people are not constrained to operate within a legal framework, then they will tend to break those agreements. If the law is structured in such a way as to reduce the likelihood that agreements will be broken, the prospects for voluntary exchange will be improved. Thus, the common law has taken a dim view of the theft of property and the breach of contract.

The normative Coase theory derives from the fact that voluntary bargaining is often costly because discovering an agreed solution might require extensive negotiation, whilst enforcing it might require monitoring and policing (Coase, 1960). For example, voluntary exchange is more likely to be successful when property rights are clear rather than when they are ambiguous. Property law therefore favours criteria for determining ownership and property rights that are clear and simple, and, for this reason, gives weight to possession and use when determining ownership.

Coase emphasised that, where there are conflicting interests, if a decision about resource use favours one party, the other party is harmed. The harm results from two incompatible activities – remove one and the harm disappears. Thus, if a factory emitting particulates into the atmosphere is located next to a laundry, there is likely to be a conflict of interest between the two. Either the factory has to incur expenditure to reduce its emissions or the laundry has to incur expenditure to ensure that its premises remain clean. Thus, losses are the result of two conflicting or interfering activities and are properly to be treated as the joint cost of both activities.

Coase's analysis also emphasises the importance of transactions costs – defined as the costs of information and bargaining, and of policing and enforcing property rights and contracts – as a principal determinant of the law's effect on economic activity and economic behaviour. Transactions costs can block mutually beneficial exchange and cooperation. Coase recognised that voluntary bargaining was often costly because discovering an agreed solution might require extensive negotiation, whilst enforcing it might require monitoring and policing. Negotiation, in particular, involves communication, and the costs of negotiation depend, in large part, upon the number of parties to the dispute and their geographical dispersion. Property law facilitates private agreements by reducing these costs.

The normative Coase theory

The normative Coase theory has wide application in law. It is of particular relevance in regulating the use of land and other natural resources. Its importance has been well illustrated by a common law judgement relating to the River Spey in Scotland (Littlechild, 1978). The judgement in question held that the owners of salmon fishing rights on the river do not have the right to prevent public use of the waters for canoeing and sailing. This decision established a property right where the situation was not previously well defined, but the resulting property right, being held by 'the public', was not transferable. Even if the value of salmon fishing, uninterrupted by canoeing and sailing, had been higher than the value of these boating activities, it is hard to see how potential fishermen could have bought the right to fish from potential boaters. Had the legal decision gone the other way, it would have been straightforward for potential boaters to negotiate with the easily identified owners of fishing rights. Far from protecting the rights of the public at large, this legal decision may well have prevented the use of the river's resources in the way most beneficial to the public. The judgement in the River Spey case had the effect of increasing transactions costs because it made it that much more difficult for competing interests to cooperate in finding a mutually acceptable solution to the problem of how to allocate access to and use of the river's resources. In other words, because property rights in the River

Spey were not tradable, it was not possible to arrive at an efficient use of the river's resources.

The choice of remedy for resolving disputes about incompatible property uses in circumstances where one person is illegitimately interfering with another person's property has been analysed by Calabresi and Melamed (1972). Where an externality has arisen, the courts have to choose between compensatory damages (or a liability rule) and an injunction (or a property rule). Where there are obstacles to cooperation, the preferred remedy is a liability rule involving the award of compensatory money damages. Where there are few obstacles to cooperation, the preferred remedy is a property rule involving the award of an injunction against the defendant's interference with the plaintiff's property. When this standard is actually applied, the preferred legal remedy depends in large part upon how many parties must participate in a settlement. Where a dispute involves a small number of contiguous property owners, the costs of private bargaining are likely to be low, bargaining is likely to be successful and, therefore, the most efficient remedy for resolving these property disputes is injunctive relief. In contrast, where disputes involve a large number of geographically dispersed individuals, the costs of bargaining will be high, bargaining will therefore not work, and the efficient legal remedy is for the courts to determine compensatory damages.

The relevance of the normative Coase theory can clearly be seen in the two principles governing the law of nuisance in England (Stephen, 1988). The first, which states the primacy of injunctive relief in English law, derives from the judgement in Pride of Derby versus British Celanese (1853). This concluded that 'if A proves that his proprietary rights are being wrongfully interfered with by B, and B intends to continue the wrong, then A is prima facie entitled to an injunction'. The second principle, which derives from Shelfer versus City of London Electric Lighting Co. (1895), concerns the circumstances under which damages (or equitable relief) rather than injunctive relief should be granted. One of these is that damages should be capable of being estimated in money terms. It is apparent, therefore, that like cost–benefit practitioners the courts have long been aware of the difficulties associated with calculating the value of environmental costs and benefits. One reason why the courts have preferred wherever possible to award injunctive relief is to allow the parties concerned the opportunity to bargain around the injunction and, in the process, reach their own judgements about the values concerned.

Easements and covenants

It is consideration of the normative Coase theory which has led to proposals to have the allocation of property rights and hence the level of environmental protection itself determined in the market (Pennington, 1998). Under proposals of this kind the role of government would be confined to the enforcement of contractual agreements made between private parties. Easements and covenants are examples of the form such voluntary trading in land development might take. An easement is defined as the legal right to use something, especially land and property, not one's own, or the legal right to prevent its owner making an inconvenient use of it. A covenant is a restriction on the use of land and property inserted in the deeds.

A system of easements can reduce uncertainty about investment in land development (Knetsch, 1983). Users of land generating nuisance in the form of pollution, etc., might be required to purchase easements from neighbouring landowners, thereby internalising the externality. The neighbouring landowners would be compensated for the loss in the value of their land, and prospective purchasers of the neighbouring land wishing to use it for a purpose that required a cessation of the nuisance-generating activity would have to buy back the easement.

Covenants, on the other hand, can be used to register publicly a restriction on the use of land. A party sensitive to a use to which a neighbour might put his land could purchase from the second party the latter's right to do what would otherwise be lawful. A party seeking a restrictive covenant would be likely to want it to 'run with the land', that is, to be binding on subsequent owners.

In principle, the scope for the use of easements and covenants is extensive. In some jurisdictions, they can actually substitute for land use planning altogether. Such an arrangement, in effect, leaves the allocation of property rights to be determined entirely by the market. Houston, Texas, would appear to be an example of such a jurisdiction, although by no means typical of American practice (Ellickson, 1973). Another example quoted in the literature is at Big Sky Valley, Montana, where developers subdivided a mountain valley, selling tracts with restrictive covenants allowing only aesthetically pleasing development (Pennington, 1998). The advantage of private solutions of this kind is that it becomes possible for consumers to reveal their demands for environmental protection and for land developers to be sensitive to individual preferences in a competitive market context (ibid.).

One proposal, attributed to Moscovitz and O'Toole (2000), is for a new system of private planning that would entail local community ownership of conservation easements and restrictive covenants through the creation of local recreation and amenity companies. Under this proposal, property owners would be free, as at present, to maintain land in its existing use and to bring forward proposals for new development. Development rights would, however, be held collectively by all the property owners in the geographical locality encompassed by a recreation and amenity company (Pennington, 2002). This proposal, which no doubt it would be sensible to try out in some localities initially on a pilot basis, would entail the state divesting itself of development rights through the establishment of local recreation and amenity companies. These companies would purchase restrictive covenants limiting new development by the participating property owners in various ways, paying for these with the issue of shares in the new company. The company board, consisting of all property owners/ shareholders, would then be responsible for decisions regarding the approval of new development. All profits and losses attributable to these decisions would be shared out in proportion to the scale of the members' holdings. Thus, the right to development land would become a form of collective property right shared by members of the company under a unified management company. Non-owning residents and others with a legitimate non-landholding interest could be included in the process by becoming company shareholders.

This proposal aims to provide a way of internalising externalities by tying the value of the proprietary community's assets directly to the decisions regarding land management within the company's jurisdiction. As such, the creation of proprietary communities could appeal to both prospective developers and local amenity interests alike. For prospective developers, company membership might bring about a greater probability of development proposals being approved. The reason is that the prospect of local residents sharing the profits would decrease the likelihood of NIMBY opposition to any form of development at all. For amenity interests, on the other hand, the creation of the recreation and amenity company would put the power to determine new development directly into the hands of those most affected by it. The property owners could negotiate contractual restrictions to ensure that any development that did take place would enhance the asset values of the company in which they held shares. This would remove the situation whereby amenity groups had nothing to gain from new development but might be forced to bear the costs in terms of environmental externalities. No doubt there would have to be a good deal of entrepreneurial experimentation by the boards of the recreation and amenity companies in order to try to discover the most desirable mix of environmental characteristics necessary to maintain a competitive edge.

The economic function of planning gain

It is important not to lose sight of the fact that an absence of arrangements to facilitate the voluntary exchange of property rights – as in the example of the River Spey – can represent an obstacle to efficient resource use. This is also true of land development rights (Fischel, 1985). A key question that anyone wishing to carry out an economic evaluation of land use planning has to address, therefore, is 'How far does the land use planning system allow for the possibility of allocative efficiency improvements through voluntary trading in land development rights?' Currently, the most obvious way in which such voluntary trading takes place in British land use planning is through the device known as 'planning gain' or 'planning obligations'. It is to this subject that we now turn.

There is some scope in the British planning system for negotiation about the wider implications of development proposals through the planning gain provision enshrined in Section 52 of the 1971 Town and Country Planning Act.[2] This introduced the concept of 'planning by agreement' whereby a local planning authority can enter into an agreement with a developer 'for the purpose of restricting or regulating the development or use of land, either permanently or during such period as may be prescribed by the agreement'. Planning gain exists when a developer obtains planning permission by providing, at his own expense, an asset or service to the community that would not have been provided but for the need to obtain planning permission. The principal benefit to be gained – planning gain – through planning by agreement is that it allows the local planning authority to obtain material benefits or control aspects of development which, if attempted by attaching conditions to planning permission, would be *ultra vires.*

There seem to be two rather different ways of looking at the economic function of planning gain. First, it might be regarded as a means by which third parties can be compensated for the damage arising from externalities generated by land development. Research carried out for the then Department of the Environment into the best practice in the use to be made of environmental statements in decision-making about planning permission advocated this view of the matter. The report stemming from the research argued that planning authorities should be more concerned about the wider costs and benefits of a development. This included, in

---

2   Now superseded by Section 106 of the 1991 Planning and Compensation Act. This introduced the concept of 'planning obligations' to replace that of 'planning gain' used in Section 52 of the 1971 act. Although the language is different, the two concepts are, to all intents and purposes, the same thing.

particular, whether or not the external environmental costs of the proposed development could be internalised, for example by compensatory payments in money or in kind to those whose interests were adversely affected (Land Use Consultants, 1994b).

One problem with this approach is that many externalities do not meet the Pigovian assumption (Pigou, 1920) of mutual recognition of effects by the damaged party and by the damaging party (Bowers, 1993). In the past, the benefits of planning gain have accrued to the local community while the externalities associated with land development may have a broader geographical impact. For example, in a major public housing and industrial development in Swale Borough, Kent, the developers were offering substantial planning gain in the form of a £60 million bond to finance a second road crossing of the Swale, a potentially substantial benefit to the local community. However, the planning application posed threats to a wildlife habitat scheduled as a Site of Special Scientific Interest (SSSI), as a Special Protection Area (SPA) and as a Ramsar-designated Wetland of International Importance (Bowers, 1992).

An alternative way of looking at planning gain is to regard it as an informal way of taxing land betterment. Historically, when Labour administrations have been in power they have sought to levy a charge on the profits made from land development, whereas Conservative administrations have generally sought to abolish such charges. Thus, although the 1947 Town and Country Planning Acts introduced a 100 per cent development charge or 'tax on betterment', there have been a number of legislative changes since that time. The most recent of these was introduced in 1985 by the then Conservative administration, which, not for the first time, abolished betterment taxation altogether. The introduction of planning gain appears to have taken some of the steam out of the political argument about betterment taxation. If the principal function of planning gain is to extract economic rent from developers, then the interest of local planning authorities focuses not so much on assessing the externalities associated with a proposed development, but rather on how financially profitable that development might be.

The reality about the true function of planning gain seems to lie somewhere between the two positions outlined above. On the one hand, local planning authorities are likely to want to ensure that proposed developments do not impose external costs on third parties in the community. On the other hand, because there exist no clear guidelines or standards against which local planning authorities are to assess externalities, and because negotiations about planning gain are generally conducted behind closed doors, the developer's liability is open-ended and is therefore likely to amount to informal betterment taxation. The dangers in this situation are twofold. First, however much the developer agrees to pay, there is always the possibility that it will be insufficient to cover the external costs of the development. Second, because planning gain is open ended, there is always the possibility, in theory if not in practice, that the developer will end up being liable for 100 per cent of development value.

Betterment taxation

Betterment taxation proved to be something of a political hot potato for a long time after the 1947 Town and Country Planning Acts were introduced. The traditional enthusiasm of Labour administrations for betterment taxation has not always translated itself into practical policy. On the other hand, Conservative administrations have tended to be ideologically opposed to any form of betterment taxation at all. Since the Conservatives abolished betterment taxation in 1985, political debate about the subject has been muted, and it is not altogether surprising therefore that betterment taxation does not feature in the Green Paper proposals. The present political truce on the subject is probably to be accounted for by two factors. First, whatever the law may say on the subject, planning gain and planning obligations have de facto operated as a kind of informal betterment tax, the proceeds of which have been used to benefit local communities. The proposals contained in the planning obligations Green Paper seem unlikely to change this. Using planning obligations to provide 'social, economic and environmental benefits to the community as a whole' implies that the authors regard it as a form of tax rather than as a compensation mechanism for internalising externalities.

Second, there remains a degree of confusion about the direction in which the proceeds from land development ought to go. For the last 50 years or so, transactions in development land in the UK have taken place on the assumption that development rights did not transfer with land unless, until and to the extent that planning permission was granted for development. Under the existing arrangements, when planning permission is granted, the development value accrues to the landowner, whereas, when planning permission is denied, it is only rarely that the landowner will be entitled to any kind of compensation. This has caused one observer to comment on what he describes as the ethical contradiction in the current position. If development value belongs to the state, as would be implied by the formal nationalisation of land development rights, then those prevented from developing their land should receive no compensation. If, on the other hand, development value is the property of owners or developers, then those who are not permitted to realise it should be compensated, and there can be no recoupment of this development value by the state (Reade, 1987).

The last part of this statement is misleading: it implies that land development rights have to be nationalised for the state to be able to recoup the development value. There are undoubtedly limits to the extent to which this is possible. However, these limits are more to do with the economics of the way the land market operates than with the question of whether land development rights are owned by the state. For example, if rates of taxation of development value are too high, one consequence is likely to be a drying up of the supply of land for development. Nevertheless, it is always open to the public authorities to recoup a proportion of development value through the tax system. To some extent, this will happen anyway through regular taxes such as corporation tax, income tax and capital gains tax. Where the yield from these taxes is deemed insufficient, there is always the possibility of introducing additional taxes. Witness the introduction of a windfall tax on the privatised utilities following the election of the Labour administration in 1997! Recouping development value is not, in the author's view, a significant argument in the debate as to the desirability or otherwise of having land development rights nationalised.

This is not to say that the taxation of land development value is itself of little or no importance. On the contrary, the existence of economic rent in the form of windfall gains resulting from changes in land values consequent upon planning decisions seems a good reason for wanting to introduce such taxes. Two examples of such planning decisions may be mentioned here. First, changes in local authority development plans in the designated use to which land may be put are an obvious source of windfall capital gain. Second, local planning authority decisions to place artificial restrictions on the number and extent of certain kinds of development, such as out-of-town shopping centres, are likely to result in supernormal profits for those fortunate enough to be able to secure planning permission for the kind of development in question. Possible ways of transferring windfall gains of this kind to the public purse would be by auctioning planning permission to the highest bidder or by inviting tenders for planning permission for particular kinds of development. In the recent past, HM Treasury has, of course, used a somewhat similar kind of policy instrument in the auctioning of mobile telephone licences.

Planning gain and ethical standards

The Green Paper on planning obligations notes the conclusion of Lord Nolan's committee that planning obligations were the most intractable aspect of the planning system with which the committee had had to deal (Committee on Standards in Public Life, 1997). Perhaps not surprisingly, the Green Paper adjudges that the present system of planning obligations is operating in a way that is inconsistent, unfair and lacking in transparency. Planning agreements are seen as taking an unacceptably long time to negotiate, involving unnecessarily high legal costs. The current system is considered to be responsible for frustrating or delaying development and even causing it to be abandoned. (This conveniently overlooks the fact that there may be very good reasons why some developments should be abandoned if the cost of internalising externalities cannot be met.)

The planning obligations Green Paper also specifically emphasises current government policy that planning obligations should never be used as a surrogate betterment levy. It draws attention to the so-called 'necessity test' that is supposed to be used to determine the acceptability of a planning obligation. This requires that planning obligations should be 'necessary', 'relevant to planning', 'directly related to the proposed development', 'fairly and reasonably related in scale and kind to the proposed development', and 'reasonable in all other respects'. About the criteria for judging such nebulous concepts as 'necessity', 'relevance', 'reasonableness', 'fairness', etc., rather little is said. However, whatever government policy may be, the planning obligations Green Paper acknowledges that the way the system actually operates has led to charges that, on the one hand, planning permission is being bought and sold and, on the other hand, that developers are being held to ransom. It also acknowledges that contributions through planning obligations are not necessarily being used for the purposes for which they were originally sought.

Annexe A of the planning obligations Green Paper goes on to consider a number of possible options for change. These include continuing with the existing policy, allowing greater flexibility to negotiate planning obligations, and replacing planning obligations with impact fees. Having examined these options in some detail, the Green Paper proposes that local authorities should, through the plan-making process, set standard tariffs whereby they would levy different rates for planning permission for different types of development. Under this proposal, the tariffs levied would contribute to meeting the cost of a range of planning objectives, including the provision of affordable housing. It is argued that the tariff approach is, by its nature, much more transparent than a system of planning obligations based on negotiated agreements. It is proposed that details of all planning obligations should be available for public inspection and that better accounting and monitoring procedures should be put in place to ensure that planning obligations are used for the purposes intended.

In future, planning obligations are to be refocused to deliver sustainable development. This is interpreted as meaning that they should be used as a mechanism to ensure that development provides social, economic and environmental benefits to the community as a whole. While the proposal to introduce a tariff approach may have merit in bringing a greater degree of openness and accountability, this statement about its role in delivering sustainable development and in providing benefits 'for the community as a whole' does not inspire confidence. Instead the Green Paper should have recognised the dual role played by planning obligations in (a) acting as a surrogate betterment tax and (b) internalising externalities arising from land development. Whatever the law may say about not using planning obligations as a surrogate betterment tax, the reality is that, to some extent, this is precisely how they have been used. It is not obvious that, if implemented, the proposals in the Green Paper would change this position. It would be better to accept that betterment has a legitimate economic function and to arrange things accordingly.

Third party rights of appeal

The lack of transparency inherent in the current arrangements for planning gain is a serious drawback. It means there is confusion about the purpose of planning gain and doubt about just how ethically the arrangements are being administered. The proposals contained in the planning obligations Green Paper, if implemented, would reduce the uncertainty arising from negotiations over planning gain between developer and local planning authority and replace it by a pre-determined schedule of payments for different types of land development. Although such a change might have its attractions in terms of greater transparency, it is important to realise that it would mean a further move away from voluntary negotiation and therefore from Coasian principles.

On the other hand, there is little doubt that the current basis for negotiation about planning gain is less than satisfactory. Although the local planning authority no doubt sees its role in such negotiations as representing the public interest, and often consults third parties likely to be affected by any proposed development, there is no possibility of third party interests actually taking part in the negotiations. This is largely a reflection of the current legal position. As we have already noted, under the 1947 Town and Country Planning Acts, a landowner has no rights of appeal in relation to planning applications likely to result in the generation of externalities that might adversely affect his property. This deficiency is discussed in the planning Green Paper.

For its purposes, the planning Green Paper defines third parties as people who have views about a planning application, whether or not they are directly affected by it. Consideration is given to the argument that there should be a right for third parties to appeal to the secretary of state against a decision by a local authority to grant planning permission. This argument is said to be that people who feel disadvantaged by a planning approval should have a comparable form of redress to those whose planning application is rejected but who have a right of appeal. The Green Paper wastes no time in pouring cold water over this argument on the grounds that such a right would not be consistent with our democratically accountable system of planning and that it could add to the costs and uncertainties of planning. The Green Paper also claims that implementing such a proposal would make planning more uncertain, legalistic and confrontational, and that it would result in further delay to investment in major developments that will already have received thorough and careful scrutiny by a local planning authority following consultation with local people. Rejecting the arguments for a third party right of appeal, the Green Paper goes on to say that the right way forward is to make the planning system more accessible and transparent and to strengthen the opportunities for community involvement throughout the process.

An obvious flaw in the planning Green Paper's argument against third party rights of appeal is that it fails adequately to maintain the distinction between those who are, and those who are not, directly affected by a planning application. Anyone, whether or not he is directly affected by a planning application, might wish to involve himself in the democratic process to which the Green Paper attaches such importance. However, the weakness of the position set out in the Green Paper is that no provision is made for those who are directly affected by planning applications and therefore have special interests to defend. Having drawn the distinction between those who are and those who are not directly affected by planning applications, as it does, the planning Green Paper then proceeds to ignore the distinction.

A further flaw in the planning Green Paper's argument is that it overlooks the principal reason for the uncertainty and confrontational nature of the existing arrangements. For example, one of the major causes of delay in planning is that, under the present system, objectors to planning applications, for example in planning inquiries, have every interest in continuing to engage in argument in an effort to get what they want. In the case of major public infrastructure projects, such as the fifth terminal at Heathrow, these arguments can drag on for years. In our view this is unlikely to change unless and until it is recognised that it is the interests of third parties directly affected by planning decisions that the planning system most needs to provide for.

At present, planning gain is the most significant way through which the rights and economic interests of third parties are addressed in the British planning system. Unfortunately, however, there is no guarantee that planning gain will result in any compensation for damage caused by land development to third parties. The planning obligations Green Paper purports to be opposed to the use of planning gain as a surrogate betterment tax. However, it is hard to see how else it can be regarded when the Green Paper itself argues that the product of planning agreements is to be used 'to deliver sustainable development' and 'to provide social, economic and environmental benefits for the community as a whole'. Providing benefits for the community at large is very different from ensuring that the interests of third parties damaged by development are properly addressed.

Logically, if the planning obligations Green Paper is opposed to the use of planning gain as a surrogate betterment tax, its authors might be expected to favour the use of planning gain to compensate third parties whose interests are damaged by development. If this were so, it would imply a view that the purpose of planning gain should be clarified so that it is specifically designed to address the problem of how best to internalise externalities. Of course, there is another possible explanation of the planning obligations Green Paper's argument. This is that the authors of the paper, despite their protestations to the contrary, do indeed see planning gain as a surrogate betterment tax and believe that it should continue to have that function. One implication for the land use planning system of such a view is that the proceeds of planning gain would continue to be used for purposes that would not necessarily redress the damage done to third parties by development. In these circumstances, planning decisions would continue to generate controversy and injustice because those decisions would continue to be at odds with the Pareto criterion.

Privatisation of land development rights

While the planning Green Paper rejects the idea of third party rights of appeal, it does not even consider the more radical proposal of privatising land development rights. Privatising land development rights does not necessarily imply adopting a free market approach to land development. The principal change would be that, in future, it would be the courts rather than the secretary of state that were the ultimate arbiter. The courts would not only be the arbiter of whether planning procedures were being properly adhered to, but also of the content of planning decisions, including the question of whether the rights of third parties were being properly protected. Here again, therefore, the focus would be on the problem of internalising externalities.

On 13 December 2000, in four separate applications, the High Court considered the English planning system and found it wanting in terms of Article 6 of the European Convention on Human Rights. The High Court found that the role of the secretary of state as the ultimate decision-maker in current planning legislation was incompatible with the procedural right to a fair hearing set out in Article 6. One consequence of this finding, if it had been upheld, was that the secretary of state would no longer have been allowed to determine planning appeals, as his doing so would have contravened the Human Rights Act. The ruling would have removed the existing conflict of interest whereby the secretary of state both sets the rules of the planning system and also decides the outcome of individual cases brought under those rules (Armstrong, 2000). So concerned was the secretary of state by this finding that he applied for leave to appeal directly to the House of Lords. If the House of Lords had upheld the High Court's ruling, institutional change in planning would have been inevitable. As it was, the House of Lords overturned the High Court's verdict. It therefore appears that legislation will now be necessary before the secretary of state can be divested of his powers in this area.

The way in which privatising land rights might work in practice can be seen from experience in the USA. There the right to develop land is protected as a private property right by the Fifth Amendment to the US Constitution, and the US Supreme Court has been taking an increasingly strong line against regulatory interference with it (Grant, 1998). The main instrument of land use planning in most jurisdictions in the USA is land use zoning (Cullingworth and Nadin, 1994). The way zoning operates under the common law is that ownership of land confers a bundle of rights, of which one is the right to develop the land provided that it does not adversely affect the property rights of others. The law of nuisance limits this right, as do individually negotiated restrictions such as easements and restrictive covenants. For each zone, regulations set out which uses or combinations of uses of land are allowed. They also prescribe standards or limitations on the physical shape of new development.[3] In most American jurisdictions, therefore, land development rights are held as private property, but the exercise of those rights is subject to regulation by the land use planning authorities.

As the planning obligations Green Paper observes, an effective planning obligations system should be transparent and provide greater certainty to all stakeholders in the planning process. To this end the Green Paper sets out three options for change: providing full flexibility within the law for local planning authorities to negotiate planning obligations; enforcing more rigorously a strict necessity test; and replacing planning obligations by impact fees. The Green Paper rejects the first of these on the grounds that it would require a strong framework to satisfy Nolan's concerns about propriety and to avoid any accusation that planning consents are being bought and sold. Impact fees, on the other hand, would apparently 'undermine the flexibility of the development control process, leading local planning authorities to refuse certain planning applications they might otherwise have been able to approve had they been able to negotiate site-specific agreements'

---

3   The economic purpose of zoning, as practised in the USA and elsewhere, has to do with the problem of how to internalise externalities. Zoning fulfils this function by separating incompatible land uses. Technically speaking, the use of zoning is justified when there is non-convexity in the production set. This is when, because of the nature and extent of the externalities generated, optimal economic efficiency is only possible when one enterprise or another is completely excluded and/or the two enterprises are kept completely separate (Cooter and Ulen, 1988). Environmental externalities from modern industrial uses are far more limited than those for which zoning – based on the separation of incompatible land uses – was originally designed. This change is reflected in the current interest, in British planning, in 'mixed use development', although zoning may still be useful, for example as a means of reducing other externalities, such as heavy traffic in residential areas (Grant, 1998).

(ODPM, 2002a). The Green Paper also argues that it would be difficult to set impact fee scales.

Of the three options considered, the Green Paper goes for the strict necessity test option, and no doubt this would be the option involving least upheaval. In reality, any of the three options might be acceptable provided they addressed the problem of internalising externalities. Unfortunately, it does not appear that this was what was in the minds of the authors. The objection to impact fees on the grounds that local planning authorities would not be able to negotiate site-specific agreements does not appear to have much force. Ideally, there would be two elements to such agreements, reflecting the cost to the authorities of installing necessary public infrastructure before development can go ahead on the one hand and the cost of internalising externalities affecting third parties on the other. The objection that it would be difficult to set impact fee scales is also questionable; it is a hurdle other jurisdictions, including, for example, the Canadian province of Ontario, have not found impossible to overcome.

Environmental impact fees

A possible way of making use of the impact fee approach would be to give legal effect to the proposals contained in the best practice guidance on the use to be made of environmental statements in the evaluation of planning applications (Land Use Consultants, 1994a,b). Under these proposals, the local planning authority would grant planning permission subject to the payment of an environmental impact fee and a public infrastructure fee. Ontario is one of a number of overseas jurisdictions to make use of impact fees to control development. In Ontario, developers compensate the local planning authority for the external costs associated with the development. The Ontario system transfers the entitlement to develop in return for a judicially determined price or impact fee (Stephen, 1987).

The basis for calculating the environmental impact fee in the UK would be the environmental statement that, under the terms of an EC Directive, already has to accompany planning applications for many categories of private and public development projects. The environmental statement would have to be vetted by the local planning authority and, as environmental statements are normally set out in terms of physical impacts, methodologies based on the techniques of environmental valuation would have to be developed to translate physical assessments of environmental damage into monetary terms.

The estimation of the public infrastructure fee, which would be used to cover the cost of providing public infrastructure such as public utilities, roads, etc., would be governed by the OECD's 'polluter pays' and 'user pays' principles.[4] This could be done by drawing on experience in North America and elsewhere in calculating impact fees[5] (see, for example, Nelson, 1988).

Under the terms of the proposal put forward here, the determination both of the environmental impact fee and also of the

4   The 'user pays' principle is a variant of the 'polluter pays' principle. Instead of the polluter paying for the cost of measures determined by the authorities to reduce emissions of pollutants, the 'user' pays for the cost of public infrastructure associated with land development.

5   Variants of the impact fee model have already been used in the UK from time to time. For example, in 1994, Northamptonshire District Council undertook, in consultation with the landowners affected, a calculation of the proportionate contributions to be made by each to local infrastructure that would be required in order to accommodate a major housing development on their land (Grant, 1998).

public infrastructure fee would be subject to judicial review. For the first time, the prospective developer would have access to the courts to challenge the content of planning decisions. This access to the courts would logically also extend to third parties; as the environmental impact fee would be designed to compensate third parties adversely affected by the proposed development, both the amount and the use made of the environmental impact fee would be of legitimate concern to them. This proposal has potential for introducing some structure, transparency and predictability into decision-making about planning permission.

The objection will doubtless be raised that British courts have no expertise in this area, which should best be left to government. This is another argument that seems to have little force. Admittedly, the courts in the UK have little, if any, experience of the use of environmental valuation techniques. Nor to date have they been willing to admit the results of environmental valuation research as evidence in court. On the other hand, it is obvious that, where they need it and where they are minded to do so, courts in other jurisdictions are perfectly capable of acquiring expertise in environmental valuation. Evidence based on environmental valuation research has long been accepted in courts in Canada and the USA. Perhaps the most celebrated example followed in the wake of the *Exxon Valdez* oil disaster when 11 million gallons of crude oil spilt into the waters of Prince William Sound, Alaska. On that occasion both the US courts and the US National Oceanic and Atmospheric Administration (NOAA) took very seriously indeed the problem of assessing the extent of the environmental damages due. NOAA set up a panel of eminent economists explicitly to advise on whether the results of contingent valuation research were robust enough for use in court proceedings (see, for example, Willis, 1995).

Environmental dispute resolution

If land development rights were privatised in the way proposed here, it would be important to have in place mechanisms that would avoid the need for continual recourse to the courts for the resolution of disputes. Litigation is expensive and there are often cheaper ways to resolve disputes about land development proposals than recourse to the courts. One way in which this can be done is by means of alternative dispute resolution mechanisms. In the case of land use planning, such mechanisms might fall into the category known as environmental dispute resolution. There is not space in this paper to provide a detailed description of the methods of environmental dispute resolution that have been developed over the last quarter of a century or so, particularly in the USA. The interested reader is referred to existing texts on the subject (see, for example, Susskind and Cruikshank, 1987). Nevertheless, it is important to recognise the potential role environmental dispute resolution can play in overcoming some of the obstacles to voluntary agreement about proposed land development.

In the USA, environmental dispute resolution has developed in response to precisely the kind of problems faced in the planning of major infrastructure projects in the UK. The key difference is that, whereas in the USA opposition to major infrastructure investment tends to manifest itself in the form of costly and time-consuming litigation, in the UK it tends to be through costly and time-consuming planning inquiries. As the Green Paper on the processing of major infrastructure projects says:

> The processing of major infrastructure projects through the
> planning system has always presented a challenge. On the
> one hand have been demands for a fair and thorough debate
> so that the views of all concerned are heard before a decision

is taken. On the other are complaints that any process which attempts to take into account all such views is bound to be so slow and costly that the economy itself is damaged ...
(DETR, 1998: 1)

In the author's view, this statement encapsulates a false dichotomy. In land use planning, there are almost bound to be disputes. Resolving them will often be costly and time-consuming. The choice to be made for policy purposes is not between having costly and time-consuming disputes and not having them. The choice is about the nature of the disputes, notably whether the planning system should aim 'to supplement and assist the market or to suspend it and put central direction in its place' (Hayek, 1960). Where the planning inquiry is conducted as a debate in which anybody who has views on the planning decision in question is able to argue their case, the ultimate outcome will be the centralised direction of planning. Where the planning inquiry is an informal negotiating process in which third parties whose interests are likely to be affected by the proposed development negotiate with the prospective developer, the outcome will be a market solution whereby externalities are effectively internalised. The author would argue strongly in favour of the latter approach. In our view, the focus of decision-making in planning should be on whether potential Pareto improvements are to be had and how compensation arrangements are to be put in place to achieve them.

5 MARKET-BASED INSTRUMENTS

Practical and theoretical advantages

An important limitation of the use of property law and private agreements in the field of land use is that, in densely populated countries like the UK, there are often too many competing interests to make meaningful negotiation and litigation possible. It is generally recognised that, where the number of individuals concerned is large, the likelihood of voluntary negotiations becomes small, because the administrative costs of coordination become prohibitively expensive[1] (Baumol and Oates, 1988). In other words, markets fail because the costs of defining and enforcing property rights – the transactions costs – are far too high. For this reason, many commentators take the view that some form of public regulation of land use is inevitable (Fischer, 1981). The counter-argument is that transactions costs are also present within the political sphere and that the alternative to markets, namely government regulation, is far from being costless and might even entail greater transactions costs (Pennington, 1996).

Although the transactions, monitoring and policing costs associated with voluntary trading are no doubt expensive, it is

---

1 A related point is that, as the number of participants becomes critically large, the individual will more and more come to treat the behaviour of others as beyond his own possible range of influence (Buchanan, 1967).

perhaps unfortunate that all too many people have been ready to assume that, in the field of land use planning, there is therefore little alternative to public regulation. Even if this assumption were justified, however, there would still be room for argument about the precise form that public regulation might take. It is, for example, easy to overlook the possible role market-based instruments – more loosely known as economic instruments – might play in land use planning. The planning Green Papers make little reference to the case for market-based instruments beyond a discussion of the possibility of varying the tariff that might be applied as part of the 'strict necessity test', as, for example, between green field and brown field sites. This is a serious omission.

The role of market-based instruments in offering a potentially more cost-effective means of delivering environmental objectives has long been advocated. Experience with their use had, more than a decade ago, led to the conclusion that the issue is no longer whether they have a role to play, but rather what kind of role they should play (Tietenberg, 1990). In the UK, their use was advocated in the 1990 environment White Paper (HM Government, 1990) and has been reiterated on various occasions since (see, for example, the second-year report on progress with the environment White Paper: HM Government, 1992). In contrast, progress in actually introducing market-based instruments in the UK has been quite slow. Although the landfill levy and the London traffic congestion charge are examples of market-based instruments that have implications for land use, there has been virtually no progress at all in the field of land use planning as such.

Market-based instruments can help to overcome the problem of externalities by attaching a price to using the environment. The normal operation of markets then ensures that environmental resources are allocated efficiently between potential users. Market-based instruments offer significant advantages over direct regulation as a means of delivering environmental objectives. They encourage cost-effectiveness, induce innovation, provide greater flexibility, generate information, and may contribute to public revenues (Department of the Environment, 1993). An important question, therefore, is how might market-based instruments be used for land use planning purposes?

In answering this question, it is important to realise that there are various different kinds of market-based instruments. Each has its own advantages and disadvantages. The two most important kinds of market-based instrument are environmental taxes and charges on the one hand and environmental trading regimes on the other. The choice between them will depend on the circumstances. For example, in the field of pollution control, where an overall pollution reduction target is in place, a system of marketable emissions permits will be more reliable in delivering it than an emissions tax. On the other hand, where this is not the case, and where the transactions costs associated with operating an emissions trading regime are high, an emissions tax might be a more attractive option (Tietenberg, 1990).

Tradable development rights (TDRs) are the equivalent of marketable emissions permits in the field of land use planning. Taxes, say on green field development, are the equivalent of pollution taxes. As with tradable emissions permits, one advantage of tradable development rights is their ability to deliver overall targets for the environment. Thus, whilst a sulphur tax is likely to result in a reduction in sulphur pollution, it will not necessarily produce some pre-determined overall sulphur pollution reduction target. Equally, whilst a differential tax regime favouring brown field rather than green field development will no doubt lead to relatively more brown field development than there might otherwise have been, it cannot guarantee some particular ratio of brown field to green field development. Potentially, this is an important advantage in favour of the use of TDRs rather than other kinds of market-based instrument in land use planning.

Urban containment as a policy objective

To illustrate the potential use of market-based instruments in land use planning, it will be convenient to do so in relation to the long-standing land use planning policy objective of urban containment. Urban containment has, historically, been to do with the prevention of urban sprawl. This seems to be regarded by government as falling into the category of what economists describe as 'merit goods'. Merit goods are those goods and services that, in the eyes of government, are somehow worth more than their market value. They are defined as those kinds of goods and services which the government decides should be produced in greater measure than people would choose to consume if left to their own devices. The term covers several possibilities as to the reasons why something might be regarded in this way. It might be because the government feels that people are not the best judges of their own best interests. It might be because it feels that production of the good in question contributes to the maintenance of certain social values that cannot be expressed in market terms. It might be because the government feels that production of the good confers positive externalities (Lipsey, 1989). For whatever reason, urban containment has long been regarded as a desirable planning objective. Evidence of this can be seen in the long-standing policy of protecting green belts around major towns and cities.

The policy of urban containment in the UK is based on the idea that a rigid distinction between the urban and the rural should be maintained (Abercrombie, 1933). Following the introduction of the 1947 Town and Country Planning Acts and also of the Agriculture Act of the same year, the policy of urban containment was manifest in the designation of special environmental and agricultural areas. These include green belts, National Parks, Areas of Outstanding Natural Beauty (AONB), etc. They also include the higher grades of agricultural land, Environmentally Sensitive Areas (ESAs), Sites of Special Scientific Interest (SSSIs), etc. No doubt these policies have, in recent years, been justified under the banners of 'sustainable development', 'biodiversity conservation', and so on, but, in essence, it is urban containment with which they are concerned. A more recent manifestation of the policy of urban containment has been the setting by government of ever higher percentage targets for the proportion of new building to be developed on brown field rather than green field sites.

Statutory land use planning designations, including green belts, National Parks, AONBs and SSSIs, accounted, by 1994, for about 46 per cent of the land area of England. In addition, by the same year, 30 per cent of English farmland was graded as the highest-quality agricultural land by the Ministry of Agriculture, Fisheries and Food and a further 30 per cent was designated as ESAs. Over 50 per cent of the land area of England is thus covered by controls which forbid all but agriculture and forestry-related developments. This compares with 11 per cent of the land area of England which is devoted to urban uses (Pennington, 1996).

At least since the time of Professor Dennison's minority report to the Scott Committee, the policy of treating urban containment as a merit good has been questioned by some on the grounds of whether the cost involved can be justified and, if so, who should be bearing that cost. This kind of approach is the one which economists tend to adopt when confronted with pre-determined policy objectives. In such circumstances, the focus of economic analysis is to determine how costly the preferred policy might be in comparison with other possible options.

The cost of running the policy of urban containment, besides the substantial element of public expenditure incurred in running the apparatus of land use planning itself, also includes conservation expenditure through a labyrinth of quangos and bureaucracies. This public expenditure is justified on the grounds that it is necessary in the interests of conserving the countryside. Public choice theory, on the other hand, recognises the importance of human self-interest and predicts that, where the motives of bureaucrats, politicians and interest groups are not constrained by institutional incentives, it is 'government failure' rather than 'market failure' which will be pervasive (McFarquhar, 1998). On this view, conservation depends on an end to bureaucratic controls and a greatly enhanced role for private individuals and voluntary bodies through the use of restrictive covenants, etc. (Pennington, 1996). Contributions to voluntary conservation bodies are, of course, less than they might be because of the free-rider problem; as there is no compulsion to contribute, it is likely that many people simply accept the benefits of the voluntary conservation sector without contributing to its costs. Nevertheless, it is easy to understate the potential role of the voluntary sector in conservation.

Impacts on land and house prices

Economists have long argued that an important cost of the policy of urban containment is that it leads to higher prices for new and existing homes, higher building densities, lower levels of new housing development, etc. For example, Evans (1999) points out that planning gain would not have been possible without the strict planning controls on developments that have caused the value of land with planning permission to be higher than its value without it. Attempts to quantify the effects of land use planning on land and house prices run up against the problem of the lack of a counter-factual: the lack of information on precisely what might have happened in the absence of strict planning controls, or with less strict planning controls.

Nevertheless, in recent years the relationship between planning and housing and land prices in England has been something of an exception to the general rule that the economics of land use planning has been relatively under-researched. Some of the leading researchers in the UK include Bramley (1999); Bramley and Watkins (1996); Cheshire and Sheppard (1989; 1996); Evans (1983; 1988); Eve (1992); Monk and Whitehead (1999); and Monk, Pearce and Whitehead (1996). Space does not permit a proper review of this research here. The interested reader may wish to look at the recent summary of the arguments and evidence provided in Chapter 9 of Adams and Watkins (2002). Suffice it to say that the results of different studies by different authors have pointed to a wide variety of possible policy responses in terms of land use planning.

A particularly suggestive, and much quoted, set of empirical studies, using data from 1984 and 1993, is that by Cheshire and Sheppard (1989; 1996). These authors undertook comparative studies of two local housing markets. As case studies, they selected Reading and Darlington, two towns with markedly different planning regimes, the former being much tighter than the latter. With a planning regime in Reading as relaxed as the one in Darlington, the reduction of housing costs in the former would have been equivalent to an increase in household income of approximately £640 per annum at the urban periphery and £775 per annum in the urban core.

The possible impact on house and land prices of land use planning policies designed to contain urbanisation was, of course, one of the consequences Professor Dennison had in mind when he wrote his minority report for the Scott Committee. It is all very well to conserve the rural environment. However, if the price to be paid for this is low-paid workers being unable to find anywhere they can afford to live, this is, or ought to be, of concern to government. The problem is that, despite the economic research that has been done, the nature and extent of the trade-off between the conservation of the rural environment on the one hand and the provision of affordable housing on the other remains only imperfectly understood.

This will doubtless not deter government ministers from making grand statements about how tens if not hundreds of thousands of new houses are 'needed' in places like 'the Thames Gateway' or 'the M11 corridor'. Such statements continue to be made regardless of the fact that, in the more desirable areas of south-east England, local planning authorities have ignored previous government diktats (*The Economist*, 2003). They also appear to ignore the fact that housing development on the scale anticipated in south-east England, if achieved, seems likely to exacerbate regional disparities in income and employment between the South-East and other parts of the country. To that extent, the development anticipated might prove self-defeating. Also, of course, the statements themselves seem to be based on the assumption that the demand for new houses is completely independent of the price to be paid for them.

The benefits of urban containment

Quite apart from the costs associated with the policy of urban containment, doubts have been expressed about the extent of the benefits associated with it (Evans, 1988; Pennington, 1996). First, it is not obvious that it is actually necessary to 'contain' urban land. Even if the extent of urban land had been expanding as rapidly since the Second World War as before it – unlikely in view of the slowdown in the rate of growth of the population – it would still account for less than 20 per cent of England's land area.

Second, the idea that somehow urban land is environmentally bad while rural land is environmentally good is, at best, an oversimplification and, at worst, a distortion of the truth. One of the most telling of environmental indicators is the population of wildlife, notably birds. Wild bird populations are at least as seriously threatened by intensive agricultural production methods stimulated by the EU's Common Agricultural Policy as they are by urban development. Probably the most powerful and far-reaching pressure against wildlife in the countryside is that produced by the extensive use of pesticides and synthetic fertilisers. Insecticides and herbicides deplete the countryside of the plants and invertebrates that form the base of complex food chains for wildlife. Fertilisers enter and pollute waterways as they are washed into them from surrounding fields (Emery, 1986). It is true that certain species of birds, such as the house sparrow, have recently been under much

85

pressure in towns and cities. However, the population of many other species of birds might have been healthier if more rather than less land had been used as suburban gardens instead of for intensive agricultural production.

Given that over 80 per cent of the British population lives in towns and cities, it is arguably more important to ensure that there is more natural green space in our cities than to preserve for ever belts of greenery on their borders (ibid.). England is one of the most densely populated countries in the world, and, for this reason, land is in short supply. Of course, there is not the same land hunger as there is in certain less developed countries where direct dependence on the land for subsistence purposes is still acute. Nevertheless, it is surely far more important for land use planning policy to concentrate on the optimal use of land than to maintain the largely artificial distinction between urban and rural land.

In the USA, research on the economics of urban containment has focused on the case for suburban development in preference to compact development in city centres (see, for example, Gordon and Richardson, 1996). Some of the issues raised are immediately recognisable in the UK context. An example is the supposed scarcity of good-quality agricultural land. Another is the long-term decentralisation of population and employment away from the large cities. The research also explores the two kinds of development pattern in terms of energy efficiency, the pattern of urban transport and telecommunications, whether compact development is equitable, etc. An evaluation of these issues did not appear to establish the case for promoting compact development. On the contrary, the research concluded that the pejorative description of suburban development as 'urban sprawl' was unjustified and unfair (ibid.).

There may be doubts about how far US research findings of this kind are applicable in the much more densely populated conditions of the UK. Land for development is in much shorter supply in the UK than in the USA, so it would be wrong simply to transfer findings relevant to the latter country to the UK context. However, it is hard, even in UK conditions, to escape from the negative connotations associated with 'urban sprawl' as an expression. It conjures up notions of urban development as some kind of unhealthy disease. A more positive-sounding policy objective that has been pursued in recent years is 'mixed-use development'. Another might be 'land use zoning'. At present, mixed-use development is regarded as something altogether different from urban containment in that it refers largely to the built environment. However, there seems no obvious reason why the concept should not be expanded to include the rural environment too. This would certainly make a good deal of sense in the context of a land use planning policy based on the objective of economic optimality. It would also make possible a land use planning policy focused on the overall pattern of development – and the zoning of different kinds of development – rather than simply on how to prevent what is currently perceived as undesirable urbanisation. In this context, development would include not simply new building but also the use to which land is put, whether for housing, agriculture, wildlife conservation, etc.

Tradable development rights in land use zoning

Whatever the doubts about the benefits of urban containment, an effective policy for achieving it has somehow to address the trade-offs involved. It might be that the opportunity cost of more new housing in the south-east of England is a loss to the rural environment and more regional congestion. Equally, it might be that the opportunity cost of conserving the rural environment and of avoiding more regional congestion is less new housing. In other words, there may well be a trade-off between housing development on the one hand and conserving the rural environment and the avoidance of further regional congestion on the other. The kind of information ideally required by land use planners fully to understand the precise nature of that trade-off is unlikely to become available for a very long time, if at all. This paucity of information is a very good reason for adopting market-based instruments. In principle, the important trade-offs in land development can be sorted out more cost-effectively by the market than by bureaucrats.

One market-based instrument with the potential to deliver an element of flexibility in land use zoning, in a manner analogous to the tradable permit in the field of pollution control, is the tradable development right (TDR). A well-known example of TDRs used for land use planning purposes is the New Jersey Pinelands in the USA (Clark and Downes, 1995). Under a system of TDRs, some areas can be specified as 'conservation zones' and others as 'development zones' or 'agricultural zones'. Land development rights are allocated to landowners in all zones, but, as development rights can be exercised only in the development zones, landowners holding development rights have either to exercise those rights in development zones or to sell them to others to do so. Development rights are therefore created only through permanent land conservation, and pressure to develop automatically stimulates permanent land conservation. The TDR system allows development in designated growth areas at a higher density than would otherwise be allowed, but it also offers a potentially cost-effective way of achieving public conservation goals.

The habitat transaction method (HTM) is a variant of the TDR. It is applied in the habitat conservation plan developed for Kern County, California. Unlike tradable development rights, the habitat transaction method does not directly prevent development on any particular piece of land. Instead, the method classifies land according to its relative habitat value, which in turn is based on ecological criteria such as the presence of endangered species. In Kern County, the plan establishes red zones of critical habitat (worth three habitat credits per acre), green zones of moderately valuable habitat (worth two credits per acre), and white zones of minimal habitat value (where there is no credit for conservation). All development is subject to a 3:1 mitigation ratio. Thus, if developers wish to build in a red zone, they must create nine conservation credits per acre, whereas development in a green zone costs six and in a white zone three conservation credits per acre. Under the HTM, therefore, every piece of land could theoretically be developed or conserved. While there is a built-in incentive to steer development away from ecologically valuable habitat, there is no absolute guarantee that critical areas will be conserved. Logically, such an absolute guarantee of conservation could not be justified unless the value of the conservation were to be regarded as infinite. Nevertheless, in Kern County such a guarantee as this has, in effect, been provided in the form of upper limits on the extent of development in red zones.

It is no accident that much of the experimentation with TDRs has taken place in the USA. Against a background that is hostile to regulatory interference with property rights, TDRs have provided a convenient means of compensating landowners for forgoing their development rights. Where landowners acquire land in the expectation of being entitled to develop it, it is appropriate that they should be compensated for the removal of that expectation. By comparison, the current position in the UK is that there is no right to develop land except in so far as the local planning authority authorises it. The introduction of TDRs in the UK therefore presupposes that land development rights will have been privatised beforehand. But, if trading is to be promoted, there also needs to be an initial restriction on the extent of development rights, and a use restriction on their exploitation. If every landowner had an unlimited right to develop, there would be no incentive for other landowners to acquire rights from those whose land is to be protected from development. And if there is no limit on the rights that an owner can acquire and exploit in his land, then there will be negative externalities for his neighbours. So the initial allocation of rights must necessarily be restricted by a floor and a ceiling (Grant, 1998).

Not least among the obstacles to introducing TDRs in the UK is that, where land development rights are surrendered by the state, they become part of the landowner's bundle of property rights. However, having been surrendered by the state, land development rights might then have to be bought back by the state in order to secure its international obligations, for example in relation to the EC Directive on the conservation of natural habitats and of wild flora and fauna. Given that compensation for land development rights that were nationalised was part of the settlement under the terms of the 1947 Town and Country Planning Acts, the political fall-out from going down this road can well be imagined.

One of the attractions of TDRs is that they can allow for the possibility of changes to the trade-off relationships. For example, under the HTM, if government decided that greater importance should be attached, say, to wildlife conservation or to housing development, or indeed to urban containment, the number of habitat credits attaching to the different kinds of zones could be modified, as could the 3:1 mitigation ratio. These are the kinds of problem that any attempt to introduce TDRs in the UK would have to address. TDRs are little different from other kinds of market-based instrument in that they would require a good deal of prior research before they could be introduced. The introduction of a sulphur pollution trading regime in the UK had to be preceded by a good deal of sophisticated planning (see, for example, London Economics, 1992). TDRs would be no different in this respect.

Taxes and levies on green field development

A somewhat simpler form of market-based instrument that might be introduced into land use planning is a tax or levy on green field development. Generally, brown field sites are more costly to develop than green field sites because of the expensive site preparations that have to be undertaken. Yet a government commitment to an increase in the proportion of brown field to green field development implies a view that the former is intrinsically more desirable. This further implies that the cost of brown field development relative to green field development needs somehow to be reduced. On the face of it, this might be achieved either by providing tax incentives for brown field development or by taxing green field developments.

Unfortunately matters may not be quite so simple. Any tax incentive for brown field development is likely to be capitalised into brown field land values (Adams and Watkins, 2002). Discussion about taxes and levies on green field development, on the other hand, has been bedevilled by a rather unproductive focus on how the proceeds might be used (ibid.). Whether a tax on green field development would actually achieve more development on brown field sites and less on green field sites remains an open question. Adams and Watkins quote the results of a theoretical review by Needham (2000). The latter suggested that, in order to have a significant effect on land use, any such tax would need to be huge and, as a result, no owner would be willing to supply land for development. Alternatively, a tax at a politically realistic rate of, say, 10 per cent of market value would have only a small effect on prices and a negligible effect on land use.

These observations do not seem to get us very far. On the one hand, it is said that the tax would need to be huge to have any impact on the pattern of land development. On the other hand, if the tax were huge, landowners would not release land for development at all. What this seems to be suggesting is that there are no intermediate positions between no development on green field sites at all and a continuation of the present rate of development on green field sites. The only conclusion one can safely draw from this is that there is uncertainty about precisely what impact a tax on green field development would actually have on the rate of green field development. In the circumstances, one can advocate more systematic research on the subject and/or a 'suck it and see' approach to the introduction of a green field levy. As we have already noted, it is often not possible to know in advance precisely what impact a tax will have. In this respect at least, tradable development rights have more appeal.

6   POLICY IMPLICATIONS

Earlier in this paper we referred to the distinction between pecuniary and technological externalities (see Chapter 4). Both are associated with land development; both are legitimate objects of policy concern. For many years, following the introduction of the 1947 Town and Country Planning Acts, pecuniary externalities associated with land development have taken the form of economic rent arising from land use planning policies that artificially restrict the supply of land. Up to 1985, this economic rent was, intermittently, the object of betterment taxation. With the introduction of Section 52 of the Town and Country Planning Act 1971, planning gain has, in effect, superseded formal betterment taxation, which was abolished finally in 1985. However, as we have seen, the function of planning gain is ambiguous; it could just as easily be regarded as a way of internalising technological externalities as a form of betterment taxation.

This is an unsatisfactory state of affairs. One of the messages of this paper is that land use planning should not only provide ways of siphoning off economic rent associated with land development; it should also, and perhaps more importantly, embody policies for internalising the technological externalities associated with it. An example of the former kind is the auctioning of planning permission. However, it is the problem of designing policies of the latter kind which has been our principal focus. In this section we summarise the principal policy implications arising from our analysis. To some extent it might be possible to pick and choose between them, but the problem of land use planning is such that there is really no reason at all why they should not run in parallel to address different problems. We have already noted, for example, that compensation using planning gain and tradable development rights can be used to achieve similar objectives in different practical circumstances.

In the field of land use planning, government policy failure offends, first, against the normative Coase theory and, second, against the Pareto criterion. The principal offence against the normative Coase theory lies in the failure of the land use planning system to provide adequate access to the courts for those whose interests are directly affected by land use planning decisions, whether they are prospective developers or third parties to land development. Without such access, the legal framework within which voluntary trading and negotiation about land development is conducted will always be inadequate. Economically inefficient land development is likely to be the consequence. We have argued that privatising land development rights would go some way towards eliminating this weakness. What this means is that, in future, the content of planning decisions rather than simply the manner in which they are arrived at would be subject to judicial review. The secretary of state would continue to be responsible for the design of the land use planning policy framework, but no longer would he also be the ultimate arbiter in relation to decisions about land development taken within that framework.

The offence against the Pareto criterion reaches far wider than land use planning policy. The Hicks–Kaldor criterion itself offends against the Pareto criterion, and it is Hicks–Kaldor which is embodied in HM Treasury's general guidance for government departments on economic appraisal and evaluation (HM Treasury, 2003). As regards land use planning, however, failure to embrace the Pareto criterion and to have in place adequate compensation mechanisms so that the gainers from land development adequately compensate the losers inevitably results in political heat and controversy. The problem of designing compensation mechanisms mirrors the problem the courts have in deciding between injunctive and equitable relief in providing remedies for legal disputes. Injunctive relief has the advantage of allowing the parties to a dispute to negotiate around the injunction and to arrive at their own assessments of the values involved. On the other hand, injunctive relief will not always be appropriate and, in awarding equitable relief, the courts have to confront the problem of how to decide on the values involved. Understandably, the courts prefer to award injunctive relief wherever possible. However, occasions on which equitable relief has to be awarded include those occasions when the costs of reaching voluntary agreement around an injunction are prohibitively expensive. This includes occasions on which there are a large number of parties involved.

There are often many parties involved in land development, and this is one of the principal justifications for the very existence of land use planning policy. It is also one of the main reasons why it is necessary for the land use planning authorities to take a view about the costs and benefits of technological externalities. In particular, they need to take a view about who gains and who loses from land development, how much they gain and lose, and how gainers are to compensate losers. In order to reach a view about the first two questions, there is really no escape from environmental impact assessment to measure physical impacts and monetary valuation to translate physical impacts into monetary terms. These seem to be obvious tasks for local planning departments and HM Planning Inspectorate in the first instance and ultimately for the courts on appeal. It goes without saying that all these bodies would need access to the right kind of expertise. They would also need powers to arrange for compensation actually to be paid.

Lest all this is thought to be asking rather a lot, it is as well to point out that the US courts now routinely admit in evidence research findings from monetary valuation exercises. However, there are some alternative possibilities. First, in the USA in particular, the informal negotiating technique known as environmental dispute resolution has had some success in resolving disputes about the planning of major infrastructure projects. A particularly exotic example, quoted by Susskind and Cruikshank (1987), is the reaching of an agreement (not subsequently implemented) to allow the construction of a new fossil-fuelled power plant in California in exchange for the planting of a new rainforest in Costa Rica! Most disputes, however, are resolved along somewhat more mundane lines, and there seems little reason why HM Planning Inspectorate's planning inquiries should not be reconstituted along environmental dispute resolution lines.

Market-based instruments were discussed in Chapter 5. The main options are environmental taxes and charges and tradable development rights. Both are intended to accomplish the internalisation of technological externalities through the market. Ideally, both kinds of instrument would be pitched at levels designed to achieve 100 per cent internalisation. However, both do present their own problems of distribution. With environmental taxes and charges, there is always the question of what should be done with the proceeds. Generally, environmentalists favour using them for

'environmentally friendly' purposes; the use of London's congestion charge to improve public transport in the capital is generally
regarded in this light.

With tradable development rights, as with tradable pollution
permits, there is always the problem of how the initial allocation
of rights is to be made. This is not the place to discuss this issue
in detail; suffice it to say that there will always be a degree of arbitrariness about this and that some environmentalists are opposed
to pollution permits precisely because of the 'right to pollute' they
confer on their owners.

In principle every opportunity should be taken for the actual
losers to be compensated rather than the proceeds being used
for some related purpose. For example, if a development leads
to noise that reduces the value of properties, the affected parties
can be compensated directly rather than the developer making
a general contribution to the finance of other local services or
environmental amenities that may benefit others as well as or
instead of the affected party. Compensating the losers themselves
has many advantages. It helps to reduce the use of the political
system to settle development matters and thus reduces the role
of 'rent-seeking' in the political system. If the environmental
compensation is not used to compensate affected groups, there
are incentives for the affected groups to use the political system
to oppose development, despite the fact that the gainer may well
be willing to compensate the loser. Furthermore, rent-seeking
behaviour will develop among people who do not lose from the
development yet stand to gain from local authorities spending
the proceeds of impact fees. If the losers are compensated by
the gainers from a planning decision, there is an incentive for
both to work out economically efficient ways to achieve their

objectives. Finally, compensation of actual losers by gainers adheres most closely to the Pareto principle, although it would
have to be accepted that not every single loser will be adequately
compensated for the subjective loss in value from a development.
There will be practical questions. How precisely should groups
representing losers be formed? How should such groups negotiate? But there will be economic incentives for both sides to behave
rationally, as both would prefer not to use the courts as a means
of settlement, as recourse to the courts would involve significant
costs.

Land use planners will doubtless ask what role in all this there
is for the local authority development plan. The answer is that the
development plan could give way to land zoning on the American
model (see Chapter 4). Land use zoning can contribute towards
the problem of internalising externalities by separating incompatible land uses. For each zone, regulations set out the details of
how land may be developed. In most American jurisdictions, land
development rights are held as private property but the exercise
of those rights is subject to these regulations. It is important that
zoning does not involve 'positive' action, determining that certain
areas will only have certain uses, which could prevent innovation
in land use and impede the pattern of land use responding to
evolving circumstances and preferences. Instead, it should involve
certain indicative prohibitions to prevent land being developed
for clearly incompatible uses. A system of tradable development
rights would of course entail land use zoning.

7 CONCLUSIONS

Many of those who argue that the land use planning system should seek to encourage more public consultation and participation question the merit of economic optimality criteria. They tend to argue that planning decisions should reflect fundamental moral judgements about the sort of values people have. They prefer this to an economic approach on the grounds that economics knows 'the price of everything and the value of nothing'. This author does not find this argument convincing.

The task of cost–benefit analysts and those adhering to economic optimality as a policy objective is precisely to discern what people's values are. They do so on the basis of the principle of consumer sovereignty. This principle embodies the essentially democratic assumption that, with well-known exceptions, each person is the best judge of his or her own interests. As such, the cost–benefit analyst aims to elicit people's values. It cannot be emphasised too strongly that he does not seek to impose those values. The land use planning system, while it purports to set great store by the consultative nature of its deliberations, cannot hope to emulate the cost–benefit analyst in this respect. By talking about 'visions of the future', the planning Green Paper flirts dangerously with the kind of utopianism that seems to have pervaded the land use planning system for far too long. Ultimately, as Karl Popper (1944) and Friedrich Hayek (1960) long ago recognised, utopianism is likely to end up reflecting the values, not of ordinary people, but of those who run the state. As such it smacks of totalitarianism.

One of the most influential reports leading up to the 1947 Town and Country Planning Acts was that of the Scott Committee. The members of this committee were evidently reluctant to address themselves to the economic questions about resource allocation that were asked during the committee's deliberations, and eventually set out in a minority report. Instead, they preferred to adhere to a policy of urban containment almost regardless of the cost involved. Over half a century later questions about the costs of urban containment are still with us. They are to do with the cost of pursuing a policy of urban containment and who is to pay that cost. Economic research on the impact of the planning system on land and house prices has, in recent years, begun to provide part of the answer to these questions.

The land use planning system in the UK now appears to have adopted 'sustainable development' as a key strategic objective. This is unfortunate in that land use planning in the UK has suffered from the pursuit of vague and ill-defined objectives for far too long. Attempts to refine this concept since the 1988 Toronto summit have shown that, not only is the concept vague and ill defined, it is also analytically redundant. This paper has, however, argued strongly that, in essence, a commitment to sustainable development should in reality imply a commitment to economic optimisation. What this means is that the land use planning system should be geared to the internalisation of externalities. There need be no great surprise about this; the internalisation of externalities, for example by application of the 'polluter pays' principle and through market-based instruments, is already central to environmental protection policy. The question is how can it be achieved in the field of land use planning?

As the courts, but apparently not the land use planning authorities, have long recognised, the pursuit of economic optimality implies the existence of a market. In our view, an economically efficient land use planning system would aim to facilitate voluntary trading in land development rights while making proper provision for the internalisation of externalities. While it is possible to point to examples, such as Houston, where land development seems successfully to internalise environmental externalities almost with a complete absence of land use planning, our principal concern has been to identify ways of introducing voluntary trading into land use planning.

Our principal proposal is for the privatisation of land development rights. This proposal recognises the need for the environmental externalities associated with land development to be internalised. As such, it requires that there be arrangements for the assessment of the value of those externalities through routine application of environmental impact assessment and environmental valuation procedures to proposed land developments. It also requires that there be a proper mechanism for arranging for the compensation of third parties adversely affected by land development. These mechanisms should include access to the courts for third parties, and a key role for the courts as the final arbiter, not just of whether planning decisions have been taken in accordance with prescribed procedures, but also of the content of those planning decisions. It also recognises the need so far as possible to reduce litigation costs by means of alternative dispute resolution procedures, notably environmental dispute resolution. Under this proposal, the dual economic functions of planning gain in taxing betterment and internalising externalities would be kept distinct. Henceforth, the function of planning gain would be to ensure that third parties whose interests were adversely affected by land development were properly compensated.

The planning obligations Green Paper, having set its face against the use of planning gain as a surrogate betterment tax, then suggests that planning gain should be used in pursuit of 'economic, social and environmental objectives for the community as a whole'. As such the authors of the Green Paper appear unwittingly to be recommending that planning obligations should be used in future as a surrogate betterment tax; in other words the Green Paper recommends precisely the opposite of what it purports to recommend! It is not our purpose to argue against land betterment taxation. On the contrary, where land use planning creates artificial scarcities, a case can be made for it. In such circumstances, we would argue for the introduction of devices, such as the auctioning of planning permission for out-of-town shopping centres, for siphoning off such supernormal profits. However, far more important in our view is that the land use planning system should get to grips with the problem of third party interests in land development. Not only is this a condition for economic efficiency in land use development, it is also a condition for reducing the political heat generated by land use planning.

REFERENCES

Abercrombie, P. (1933), *Town and Country Planning*, London: Butterworth

Adams, D. and C. Watkins (2002), *Greenfields, Brownfields and Housing Development*, Oxford: Blackwell Science

Armstrong, L. (2000), 'Planning Appeals', letter to *The Times*, 21 December

Barzel, Y. (1989), *Economic Analysis of Property Rights*, Cambridge: Cambridge University Press

Baumol, W. J. (1965), *Economic Theory and Operations Analysis*, 2nd ed., New Jersey: Prentice Hall

Baumol, W. J. and W. E. Oates (1988), *The Theory of Economic Policy*, 2nd ed., Cambridge: Cambridge University Press

Beckerman, W. (1995), *Small Is Stupid: Blowing the Whistle on the Greens*, London: Duckworth

Bowers, J. (1992), 'The Economics of Planning Gain: A Re-appraisal', *Urban Studies*, 29(8)

Bowers, J. (1993), 'Conspectus on Valuing the Environment', *Journal of Environmental Planning and Management*, 36(1)

Bramley, G. (1999), 'Housing market adjustment and land supply constraints', *Journal of Environment and Planning A*, 37: 1,169–88

Bramley, G. and C. Watkins (1996), *Steering the Housing Market:*

New Housing Supply and the Changing Planning System, Bristol: Policy Press

Buchanan, J. M. (1967), 'Cooperation and Conflict in Public-Goods Interaction', *Western Economic Journal*, 5: 109–21

Calabresi, G. and A. D. Melamed (1972), 'Property Rules, Liability Rules and Inalienability: One View of the Cathedral', *Harvard Law Review*, 85(6): 1,089–128

Cheshire, P. and S. Sheppard (1989), 'British planning policy and access to housing: some empirical estimates', *Urban Studies*, 26: 469–85

Cheshire, P. and S. Sheppard (1996), 'On the price of land and the value of amenities', *Economica*, 62: 247–67

Clark, D. and D. Downes (1995), 'What price biodiversity? Economic incentives and biodiversity conservation in the United States', Washington, DC: Center for Environmental Law

Coase, R. H. (1960), 'The Problem of Social Cost', *Journal of Law and Economics*, 3(1): 1–44

Commission on the Third London Airport (1971), Report, London: HMSO

Committee on Land Utilisation in Rural Areas (1941), Final Report (Scott Report), Cmnd. 6378, London: HMSO

Committee on New Towns (1942), Final Report (Reith Report), Cmnd. 6876, London: HMSO

Committee on Standards in Public Life (1997), Third Report, Cm. 3702-1, London: HMSO, July

Cooter, R. and T. Ulen (1988), *Law and Economics*, London: HarperCollins

Corkindale, J. (1998), *Reforming Land-Use Planning: Property Rights Approaches*, IEA Studies on the Environment No. 12, London: Institute of Economic Affairs

Corkindale, J. (1999), 'Land development in the United Kingdom: private property rights and public policy objectives', *Journal of Environment and Planning A*, 31(11)

Cullingworth, J. B. (1997) *Planning in the USA: Policies, issues and processes*, London and New York: Routledge

Cullingworth, J. B. and V. Nadin (1994), *Town and Country Planning in Britain*, 11th ed., London: Routledge

Department of Land Economy, University of Cambridge (1995), 'Developing Indicators and Measures for Evaluating the Effectiveness of Land Use Planning', unpublished paper

Department of the Environment (1988a), 'The Green Belts', London: HMSO

Department of the Environment (1988b), 'A Perspective by the United Kingdom on the Report of the World Commission on Environment and Development', London: DOE

Department of the Environment (1991), 'Policy Appraisal and the Environment', London: HMSO

Department of the Environment (1993), 'Making Markets Work for the Environment', London: HMSO

DETR (Department of the Environment, Transport and the Regions) (1998), 'Modernising Planning', London: DETR.

DTLR (Department for Transport, Local Government and the Regions) (2001), Planning Green Paper, 'Planning: Delivering a Fundamental Change', London: DTLR

Economist, The (2003), 'Brave New Homes', 8 February, p. 36

Ellickson, R. C. (1973), 'Alternatives to Zoning: Covenants, Nuisance Rules and Fines as Land Use Controls', *University of Chicago Law Review*, 40(4): 681–781

Emery, M. (1986), *Promoting Nature in Cities and Towns*, London: Croom Helm

Evans, A. W. (1983), 'The determinants of the price of land', *Urban Studies*, 20: 119–29

Evans, A. W. (1985), *Urban Economics: An Introduction*, Oxford: Blackwell

Evans, A. W. (1988), *No Room! No Room! The Costs of the British Town and Country Planning System*, Occasional Paper 79, London: Institute of Economic Affairs

Evans, A. W. (1999), 'The land market and government intervention', in E. S. Mills and P. Cheshire (eds), *Handbook of Regional and Urban Economics*, Amsterdam: Elsevier

Eve, G. (1992), *The Relationship between House Prices and Land Supply*, London: HMSO

Fischel, W. A. (1985), *The Economics of the Zoning Laws: A Property Rights Approach to American Land Use Controls*, Baltimore, MD: Johns Hopkins University Press

Fischer, A. C. (1981), *Resource and Environmental Economics*, Cambridge: Cambridge University Press

George, H. (1879), *Progress and Poverty*, New York: Schalkenbach Foundation, 1992, originally published 1879

Gibbs, D. C., J. Longhurst and C. Braithwaite (1998), 'Struggling with sustainability: weak and strong interpretations of sustainable development within local authority policy', *Journal of Environment and Planning A*, 30: 1,351–65

Gordon, P. and H. W. Richardson (1996), 'The Case for Suburban and against Compact Development', unpublished paper

Grant, M. (1988), 'Forty Years of Planning Control: The Case for the Defence', The Denman Lecture, Department of Land Economy, University of Cambridge

Grant, M. (1996), 'If Tigard Were an English City: Exactions Law in England Following the Tesco Case', in D. Callies (ed.),

Takings: Land Development Conditions and Regulatory Takings after Dolan and Lucas, Chicago: American Bar Association

Grant, M. (1998), 'Commentary', in J. Corkindale, *Reforming Land Use Planning: Property Rights Approaches*, IEA Studies on the Environment No. 12, London: Institute of Economic Affairs

Grove-White, R. (1997), 'The environmental "valuation" controversy: observations on its recent history and significance', in J. Foster (ed.), *Valuing Nature? Ethics, Economics and the Environment*, London: Routledge, pp. 21–31

Hall, P., H. Gracey, R. Drewett and R. Thomas (1973), *The Containment of Urban England*, London: George Allen and Unwin

Hayek, F. A. (1960), *The Constitution of Liberty*, London: Routledge

Hicks, J. R. (1939), 'The Foundation of Welfare Economics', *Economic Journal*, 49(4)

HM Government (1953), 'London's Airports', Cm. 8902, London: HMSO, July

HM Government (1990), 'This Common Inheritance: Britain's Environmental Strategy', Cm. 1200, London: HMSO

HM Government (1992), 'This Common Inheritance: The Second Year Report', Cm. 2086, London: HMSO

HM Treasury (2003), 'The Green Book: Appraisal and Evaluation in Central Government', London: TSO

Hobbes, T. (1651), *Leviathan*, New York: W. W. Norton, 1997, originally published 1651

Kaldor, N. (1939), 'Welfare Comparisons of Economics and Interpersonal Comparisons of Utility', *Economic Journal*, 49(3)

Knetsch, J. L. (1983), *Property Rights and Compensation: Compulsory Acquisition and Other Losses*, Canada: Butterworth

Land Use Consultants (1994a), 'Good Practice on the Evaluation of Environmental Information for Planning Projects', Department of the Environment Planning Research Programme, London: HMSO

Land Use Consultants (1994b), 'The Research Report', Department of the Environment Planning Research Programme, London: HMSO

Lichfield, N. (1996), *Community Impact Evaluation*, London: UCL Press

Lipsey, R. G. (1989), *An Introduction to Positive Economics*, 7th ed., London: Weidenfeld and Nicolson

Littlechild, S. C. (1978), *The Fallacy of the Mixed Economy: An Austrian Critique of Economic Thinking and Policy*, Hobart Paper 80, London: Institute of Economic Affairs

London Economics (1992), 'The Potential Role of Market Mechanisms in the Control of Acid Rain', Department of the Environment, Environmental Economics Research Series, London: HMSO

McFarquhar, A. (1998), 'Environment Valuation, Project Appraisal and Political Consensus', European Society of Ecological Economics, Fifth Conference, Geneva, 4–7 March

Monk, S. and C. Whitehead (1999), 'Evaluating the impact of planning controls in the UK – some implications for housing', *Land Economics*, 75: 74–93

Monk, S., B. Pearce and C. Whitehead (1996), 'Planning, land supply and house prices', *Journal of Environment and Planning A*, 28: 495–511

Moscovitz, K. and R. O'Toole (2000), *New Incentives for Rural Communities*, Portland, OR: The Thoreau Institute

Needham, B. (2000), 'Land taxation, development charges, and the effects on land-use', *Journal of Property Research*, 17: 397–423

Nelson, A. C. (ed.) (1988), *Development Impact Fees*, Chicago, IL: Planners Press

ODPM (Office of the Deputy Prime Minister) (2002a), 'Planning Obligations: Delivering a Fundamental Change', London: ODPM

ODPM (2002b), 'Planning Policy Guidance Note 1: General Policy and Principles', London: HMSO

ODPM (2002c), 'Sustainable Communities – Delivering through Planning', London: ODPM

Pareto, V. (1927), *Manuel d'économie politique*, 2nd ed., Paris: Girand

Pearce, B. J. (1992), 'The Effectiveness of the British Land-use Planning System', *Town Planning Review*, 63(1)

Pearce, D. W. (2002), 'Saving the World with Environmental Economics: Steps Forward, Steps Back', paper presented at '10 Years in Environmental Economics: Observations from the Frontlines', seminar held on 26 November 2002 to celebrate the 10th anniversary of eftec

Pearce, D. W., A. Markandya and E. Barbier (1989), *Blueprint for a Green Economy*, London: Earthscan

Pennington, M. (1996), *Conservation and the Countryside: By Quango or Market?*, IEA Studies on the Environment No. 6, London: Institute of Economic Affairs

Pennington, M. (1998), 'Commentary', in J. Corkindale, *Reforming Land-Use Planning: Property Rights Approaches*, IEA Studies on the Environment No. 12, London: Institute of Economic Affairs

Pennington, M. (2002), *Returning Planning to the Market: An Agenda for Private Land Use Control*, Current Controversies No. 11, London: Institute of Economic Affairs

Pigou, A. C. (1920), *The Economics of Welfare*, London: Macmillan

Popper, K. (1944), *The Open Society and Its Enemies*, London: Routledge

Reade, E. (1987), *British Town and Country Planning*, Milton Keynes: Open University Press

Rowthorn, B. and H. Chang (1993), 'Public Ownership and the Theory of the State', in T. Clarke and C. Pitalis (eds), *The Political Economy of Privatisation*, London: Routledge

Royal Commission on the Distribution of the Industrial Population (1940), Report (Barlow Report), Cmnd. 6153, London: HMSO

Smith, A. (1776), *An Enquiry into the Nature and Causes of the Wealth of Nations*, London: Dent and Sons

Steele, D. R. (1992), *From Marx to Mises*, La Salle: Open Court

Stephen, F. H. (1987), 'Property Rules and Liability Rules in the Regulation of Land Development: An Analysis of Development Control in Great Britain and Ontario', *International Review of Law and Economics*, 7: 33–49

Stephen, F. H. (1988), *The Economics of the Law*, London: Wheatsheaf Books

Susskind, L. and J. Cruikshank (1987), *Breaking the Impasse: Consensual Approaches to Resolving Public Disputes*, New York: Basic Books

Tate, J. (1994), 'Sustainability: a case of back to basics?', *Planning Practice and Research*, 9(4): 367–79

Tietenberg, T. H. (1990), 'Economic Instruments for Environmental Regulation', *Oxford Review of Economic Policy*, 6: 17–31

Viner, J. (1931), 'Cost Curves and Supply Curves', reprinted in G. J. Stigler and K. E. Boulding (eds) (1952), *Readings in Price*

Theory, Chicago: American Economic Association

Von Mises, L. (1949), *Human Action*, New Haven, CT: Yale University Press

Wakeford, R. (1990), *American Development Control: Parallels and Paradoxes from an English Perspective*, London: HMSO

Willis, K. G. (1995), 'Contingent Valuation in a Policy Context: The National Oceanic and Atmospheric Administration Report and Its Implications for the Use of Contingent Valuation Methods in Policy Analysis in Britain', in K. G. Willis and J. T. Corkindale (eds), *Environmental Valuation: New Perspectives*, Wallingford, Oxon: CAB International

Willis, K. G., G. Nelson, A. Bye and G. Peacock (1992), 'Urban Development in the Rural Fringe: A Decision Analytical Framework and Case Study of the Newcastle Green Belt', ESRC Countryside Change Initiative, Working Paper 31, University of Newcastle-upon-Tyne

Willis, K. G. and M. Whitby (1985), 'The Value of Green Belt Land', *Journal of Rural Studies*, 1(2): 147–62

World Commission on Environment and Development (1987), *Our Common Future* (The Brundtland Report), Oxford: Oxford University Press

ABOUT THE IEA

The Institute is a research and educational charity (No. CC 235 351), limited by guarantee. Its mission is to improve understanding of the fundamental institutions of a free society with particular reference to the role of markets in solving economic and social problems.

The IEA achieves its mission by:

- a high-quality publishing programme
- conferences, seminars, lectures and other events
- outreach to school and college students
- brokering media introductions and appearances

The IEA, which was established in 1955 by the late Sir Antony Fisher, is an educational charity, not a political organisation. It is independent of any political party or group and does not carry on activities intended to affect support for any political party or candidate in any election or referendum, or at any other time. It is financed by sales of publications, conference fees and voluntary donations.

In addition to its main series of publications the IEA also publishes a quarterly journal, *Economic Affairs*, and has two specialist programmes – Environment and Technology, and Education.

The IEA is aided in its work by a distinguished international Academic Advisory Council and an eminent panel of Honorary Fellows. Together with other academics, they review prospective IEA publications, their comments being passed on anonymously to authors. All IEA papers are therefore subject to the same rigorous independent refereeing process as used by leading academic journals.

IEA publications enjoy widespread classroom use and course adoptions in schools and universities. They are also sold throughout the world and often translated/reprinted.

Since 1974 the IEA has helped to create a world-wide network of 100 similar institutions in over 70 countries. They are all independent but share the IEA's mission.

Views expressed in the IEA's publications are those of the authors, not those of the Institute (which has no corporate view), its Managing Trustees, Academic Advisory Council members or senior staff.

Members of the Institute's Academic Advisory Council, Honorary Fellows, Trustees and Staff are listed on the following page.

The Institute gratefully acknowledges financial support for its publications programme and other work from a generous benefaction by the late Alec and Beryl Warren.

Other papers recently published by the IEA include:

WHO, What and Why?

Transnational Government, Legitimacy and the World Health Organization
Roger Scruton
Occasional Paper 113; ISBN 0 255 36487 3
£8.00

The World Turned Rightside Up

A New Trading Agenda for the Age of Globalisation
John C. Hulsman
Occasional Paper 114; ISBN 0 255 36495 4
£8.00

The Representation of Business in English Literature

Introduced and edited by Arthur Pollard
Readings 53; ISBN 0 255 36491 1
£12.00

Anti-Liberalism 2000

The Rise of New Millennium Collectivism
David Henderson
Occasional Paper 115; ISBN 0 255 36497 0
£7.50

Capitalism, Morality and Markets

Brian Griffiths, Robert A. Sirico, Norman Barry & Frank Field
Readings 54; ISBN 0 255 36496 2
£7.50

A Conversation with Harris and Seldon

Ralph Harris & Arthur Seldon
Occasional Paper 116; ISBN 0 255 36498 9
£7.50

Malaria and the DDT Story

Richard Tren & Roger Bate
Occasional Paper 117; ISBN 0 255 36499 7
£10.00

A Plea to Economists Who Favour Liberty: Assist the Everyman

Daniel B. Klein
Occasional Paper 118; ISBN 0 255 36501 2
£10.00

Waging the War of Ideas

John Blundell
Occasional Paper 119; ISBN 0 255 36500 4
£10.00

The Changing Fortunes of Economic Liberalism

Yesterday, Today and Tomorrow

David Henderson

Occasional Paper 105 (new edition); ISBN 0 255 36520 9

£12.50

The Global Education Industry

Lessons from Private Education in Developing Countries

James Tooley

Hobart Paper 141 (new edition); ISBN 0 255 36503 9

£12.50

Saving Our Streams

The Role of the Anglers' Conservation Association in Protecting English and Welsh Rivers

Roger Bate

Research Monograph 53; ISBN 0 255 36494 6

£10.00

Better Off Out?

The Benefits or Costs of EU Membership

Brian Hindley & Martin Howe

Occasional Paper 99 (new edition); ISBN 0 255 36502 0

£10.00

Buckingham at 25
Freeing the Universities from State Control
Edited by James Tooley
Readings 55; ISBN 0 255 36512 8
£15.00

Lectures on Regulatory and Competition Policy
Irwin M. Stelzer
Occasional Paper 120; ISBN 0 255 36511 X
£12.50

Misguided Virtue
False Notions of Corporate Social Responsibility
David Henderson
Hobart Paper 142; ISBN 0 255 36510 1
£12.50

HIV and Aids in Schools
The Political Economy of Pressure Groups and Miseducation
Barrie Craven, Pauline Dixon, Gordon Stewart & James Tooley
Occasional Paper 121; ISBN 0 255 36522 5
£10.00

The Road to Serfdom
The Reader's Digest *condensed version*
Friedrich A. Hayek
Occasional Paper 122; ISBN 0 255 36530 6
£7.50

Bastiat's *The Law*
Introduction by Norman Barry
Occasional Paper 123; ISBN 0 255 36509 8
£7.50

A Globalist Manifesto for Public Policy
Charles Calomiris
Occasional Paper 124; ISBN 0 255 36525 X
£7.50

Euthanasia for Death Duties
Putting Inheritance Tax Out of Its Misery
Barry Bracewell-Milnes
Research Monograph 54; ISBN 0 255 36513 6
£10.00

Liberating the Land

The Case for Private Land-use Planning
Mark Pennington
Hobart Paper 143; ISBN 0 255 36508 x
£10.00

IEA Yearbook of Government Performance 2002/2003

Edited by Peter Warburton
Yearbook 1; ISBN 0 255 36532 2
£15.00

Britain's Relative Economic Performance, 1870– 1999

Nicholas Crafts
Research Monograph 55; ISBN 0 255 36524 1
£10.00

Should We Have Faith in Central Banks?

Otmar Issing
Occasional Paper 125; ISBN 0 255 36528 4
£7.50

The Dilemma of Democracy
Arthur Seldon
Hobart Paper 136 (reissue); ISBN 0 255 36536 5
£10.00

Capital Controls: a 'Cure' Worse Than the Problem?
Forrest Capie
Research Monograph 56; ISBN 0 255 36506 3
£10.00

The Poverty of 'Development Economics'
Deepak Lal
Hobart Paper 144 (reissue); ISBN 0 255 36519 5
£15.00

Should Britain Join the Euro?
The Chancellor's Five Tests Examined
Patrick Minford
Occasional Paper 126; ISBN 0 255 36527 6
£7.50

Post-Communist Transition: Some Lessons
Leszek Balcerowicz
Occasional Paper 127; ISBN 0 255 36533 0
£7.50

A Tribute to Peter Bauer
John Blundell et al.
Occasional Paper 128; ISBN 0 255 36531 4
£10.00

Employment Tribunals
Their Growth and the Case for Radical Reform
J. R. Shackleton
Hobart Paper 145; ISBN 0 255 36515 2
£10.00

Fifty Economic Fallacies Exposed
Geoffrey E. Wood
Occasional Paper 129; ISBN 0 255 36518 7
£12.50

A Market in Airport Slots
Keith Boyfield (editor), David Starkie, Tom Bass & Barry Humphreys
Readings 56; ISBN 0 255 36505 5
£10.00

Money, Inflation and the Constitutional Position of the Central Bank
Milton Friedman & Charles A. E. Goodhart
Readings 57; ISBN 0 255 36538 1
£10.00

railway.com
Parallels between the early British railways and the ICT revolution
Robert C. B. Miller
Research Monograph 57; ISBN 0 255 36534 9
£12.50

The Regulation of Financial Markets
Edited by Philip Booth & David Currie
Readings 58; ISBN 0 255 36551 9
£12.50

Climate Alarmism Reconsidered
Robert L. Bradley Jr
Hobart Paper 146; ISBN 0 255 36541 1
£12.50

Government Failure: E. G. West on Education
Edited by James Tooley & James Stanfield
Occasional Paper 130; ISBN 0 255 36552 7
£12.50

Waging the War of Ideas
Second edition
John Blundell
Occasional Paper 131; ISBN 0 255 36547 0
£12.50

Corporate Governance: Accountability in the Marketplace
Elaine Sternberg
Second edition
Hobart Paper 147; ISBN 0 255 36542 X
£12.50

To order copies of currently available IEA papers, or to enquire about availability, please contact:

Lavis Marketing
IEA orders
FREEPOST LON21280
Oxford OX3 7BR

Tel: 01865 767575
Fax: 01865 750079
Email: orders@lavismarketing.co.uk

The IEA also offers a subscription service to its publications. For a single annual payment, currently £40.00 in the UK, you will receive every title the IEA publishes across the course of a year, invitations to events, and discounts on our extensive back catalogue. For more information, please contact:

Subscriptions
The Institute of Economic Affairs
2 Lord North Street
London SW1P 3LB

Tel: 020 7799 8900
Fax: 020 7799 2137
Website: www.iea.org.uk